Kay's Ark

Kerry Darbishire

Kay's Ark

Kerry Darbishire

H
HANDSTAND PRESS

H
HANDSTAND PRESS

Published by Handstand Press

East Banks, Dent, Sedbergh. Cumbria.

LA10 5QT

www.handstandpress.net

First Published in 2016

Designed & set by Russell Holden - Pixel Tweaks, Ulverston
www.pixeltweakspublications.com

Printed in Great Britain by Biddles, Kings Lynn, Norfolk.

ISBN: 978-0-9576609-5-3

In memory of my mother
Kay Callaghan
1917-2005
and for her family

'In memory everything seems to happen to music.'
— Tennessee Williams

Mum and Kim on Thrang Fell 1962

In my Mother's Diary

Identifying the stems, leaves and flowers
is almost impossible — all laced to pale brown, brittle
and flaked into Autumn 1964.

Looking for a meaning, careful
not to break her days — their disarrangements
pressed as far as October, I picture her
clear as these blooms used to be —

harebell, clover, vetch, fern, edging
old tracks, slow-grazing flocks in dawn mist.
She's striding out to catch the first scents
brushed from overblown slopes, quietly

slipping the morning into her rucksack
like a map. She waits for sun
to flint the Pikes, fire bracken back to life,
unwind slate routes through crags and ghylls

trying to make sense of it.
In childish hope I smell the frail reminders
as if to tease out the yellow, blue
and green of them.

PART ONE

PART TWO

PART THREE

Preface

My earliest memory of my mother is of her voice, clear and warm as a spring day. I was nearly two years old and we'd just moved from London to Rosewood, Skelwith Bridge. I remember sitting in my pram and must have thrown a toy out because leaning over the edge to find it, the ground seemed a very long way down. Water trickled over bright green moss into a drain. We were outside the bottom gate on the roadside. I don't remember the cars but I do remember birdsong and the constant sound of the river like music forever playing. It was warm and the air was sweet with azaleas and pine. Perhaps we were going for a walk over the bridge and around the village, I don't know. Everything was new, I didn't feel afraid, just happy and safe. It was more than sixty years ago.

Mum spoke very little about her past and I dared not ask too much for fear of opening up painful wounds – which, because of her evasiveness, were surely there. After the age of five I became acutely aware of her emotions. When she was happy she'd play the piano and sing well-known ditties; but sometimes I would see a deep sadness in her face, she would speak quietly, slow then fall silent as if a dark shadow had drawn over certain episodes of her life. Why had her privileged upbringing, and her promising career in theatre, taken such an unexpected turn? Why had she escaped London and Dad to live in the Lake District? How did she manage to make a living in a quiet little village, find the strength to rise above her difficulties and eventually come to save the lives of thousands of animals? My love and admiration for my mother has driven me to dig deep and answer these questions. I want her life to make sense – to understand the things we were too young to notice or ignored, even at the risk of unearthing something she didn't want me to know.

· PART ONE ·

CHAPTER ONE

HOLLOW OAK

I remember the gravel-crunch as I swung the car round into the parking circle, hoping to avoid the sign above the door: HOLLOW OAK NURSING HOME. But a look on her face told me she knew. I tried to keep the day uplifted – spoke in a light, positive way.

'This is just until you get better, Mum,' I said. We carried her few clothes in and along the corridor to her newly-painted room. Mum was no fool, and that day showed no signs of forgetfulness.

Tony, the owner of the home, came in and sat alongside her on the single pink counterpaned bed. "This is your home now, Kay. Whatever you need, just call us. The cats will come and see you soon."

The room was fresh and bright. From a soft winged chair she would be able to see a lovely view of the garden towards the old beeches and oaks across the valley. If it rained she could watch television, listen to music or read her favourite animal books, including *My Family and other Animals* by Gerald Durrell. Mum looked up at the ceiling and along each wall, inspecting her new surroundings.

'This is like going back to boarding school,' she said, her hands pressing the mattress. I re-assessed the ornaments like fond memories we'd arranged on a shelf and side table a few days earlier with all the photos of her dogs – Kim, Jess and other four-legged companions, and the china and wood-carved gifts given throughout the years by her children, grandchildren and friends. But seeing Mum's knick-knacks here felt strange, out of context, just didn't feel right, as if I'd betrayed her. How was I going to leave her here?

My drive home was the worst. I wept all the way to Newby Bridge, up and over Gummer's Howe, down past Strawberry Bank and through Kendal. As soon as I could, I rang her on her new number. She sounded calm. Was she still protecting me, using her acting skills? She was good at that. I remembered how they used to surface in order to hide her feelings.

I couldn't sleep that night for wanting to see her again, even though Tony had told me not to return too soon. "Let her settle in." Were his words. I was racked with guilt. In the space of a few weeks, I had become the mother – faced with her private affairs, her home Rosewood, her beloved dog Bob, and three remaining cats. I wondered how she would manage without them, without the sound of the river?

* * *

It's late September, 2003. My brother Patrick, sister Judith and myself are at Rosewood. Like us, the house is quiet and raw – a strange silence without Mum. We draw back the red frayed curtains, let in faint sunshine, put on the kettle and light a fire. Numbed, we gaze at reflected flames darting the gloomy timber-clad walls, the piano, Granny's corner cupboard, heaps of books, papers: in fact, eighty-five years stuffed in drawers, thrown in the bottom of her wardrobe and sprawled around the bedroom floor. It looks like a scattered jigsaw – a life waiting to be sorted into keeping, burning, recycling. We begin ploughing through stacks of sheet music, all the pieces I remember her playing on the piano every day. We woke and went to sleep to the sound of Beethoven, Chopin, Debussy, Liszt – I'm sure a gift inherited from her great-uncle.

CHAPTER TWO

FREDERICK DELIUS

I'd heard the name Frederick Delius mentioned in conversations between the grown-ups – that he was a well-known composer and also Mum's great-uncle. When I looked further, in a book I was given called *Frederick Delius – Memories of My Brother*, written in 1935 by his sister Clare Delius, I found that his father, Julius Delius, born in 1821, came from Bielefeld, Germany and, 'under the impulse of the discovery that money could be made out of wool', came to Bradford, England in 1850. He went back to Bielefeld to marry Fraulein Elise Pauline Kroenig in 1855, then they both returned, settling in Brontë country – at Claremont House, Bradford, where in 1862 Frederick was born.

A young Frederick Delius

Julius was apparently a strict yet charitable father and founder member of the Bradford Children's Hospital. He had a real love of music, and although unable read a note he could play anything by ear. Charles Hallé, not yet Sir Charles, and his wife, the famous violinist Madame Norman Neruda, made a big impact in Bradford during that time of the first inauguration of the Hallé concerts, and as Julius was a member of the Committee of Management, they became great friends.

Julius and Elise had a large family of ten girls and four boys: Ernest, Elise, Minnie Anna, Frederick, Rose, Max, Clare, Willy, Lucy, Marguerita, Hedwig, Lily, Theodora and Elfreda (the last two died

Minnie Anna Hickling with Edith Elise

in infancy). Frederick was expected to follow in his father's footsteps and work in the wool business but instead, being intensely musical, he studied violin and as a small boy, like his father, played piano by ear and attended many concerts. Passionate about music, he visualised marvellous scenes – the sea, flocks of birds, and later, sunsets in the tropics – as he composed. His father encouraged him and at fifteen he began learning the piano, but hated repeatedly practising scales until one day he heard Chopin's 'Funeral March'. His sister Clare wrote, 'In a very agony of emotion he caught hold of the man who had played it and besought him to teach him music, especially that piece.' Thereafter he composed many beautiful pieces, including 'On Hearing the First Cuckoo in Spring' and 'The Walk to the Paradise Garden'. (As a child I heard these pieces played often and they became familiar.)

Frederick's sister, Minnie Anna, married Mum's Grandfather, Arthur William Hickling (1858-1934), a wine merchant. At first they lived at College Villas, 34 Regent Street, Nottingham. They then moved into Adbolton Hall, West Bridgford in Nottingham, where Arthur bred racehorses. Auntie Joan told me that this grand abode later became the County Hospital and eventually a nursing home.

William and Minnie had two daughters and a son: Mum's mother Edith Elise, Theodora Mary (who became the Honorable Lady Maxwell) and Harold Hickling, who became Vice Admiral during World War One (and who happened to write the book *Freshwater Admiral: Fishing the Tongariro River and Lake Taupo* based on his exploits in New Zealand.)

Minnie Anna Hickling

As dusk closes in, the first jumble of musty photos, birth certificates and letters have surfaced. I begin to see similarities – threads between Mum and her great-uncle Frederick. For a start, they were sensitive, highly musical, and both settled on the banks of a river – Brathay and Grez-sur-Loing. I tinkle around on her piano, now stiff and very out of tune – the result of years of dog and cat hairs clogging the soundboard. I remember the dogs leaping up to bark through the window at passers by, and the cats curled up inside.

I want to take Bob for a walk before it gets too dark, but he won't come, not without his Mum. I feed him and the two cats. Jester is purring and seems content but Snowdrop is skeletal and desperately needs veterinary care. I wrap the fireguard around the dying ashes. Framed between two cats keeping warm on the mantelpiece, Edith Elise Smith – Granny – watches me. Elegant as always, dressed in a two-piece suit with, clipped to her lapel, a sparkly pince-nez which, with one smooth flick of her wrist, she'd unclip and be poised to read. It fascinated me and I constantly wanted to play with it but wasn't allowed. Her short, snowy-thick hair was brushed thoroughly every night: 'Keeps hair healthy and tidy,' she used to say.

Granny was commanding, didn't mince her words, and we all knew when she meant business – often pulling us up on manners and social etiquette. Her sharp green eyes missed nothing. She walked with a spring in her step and we were encouraged to follow suit, but at the time found it pointless. Mum always spoke of and treated her with the greatest respect. As a child I recognised a formality between them. A thorough clean-up and fuss was made whenever she visited, and we had to be on our best behaviour.

I've done enough for one day. I close the curtains, turn off the lights, lock the front door and walk out into the cold night thinking about how times have changed, how Mum's life and mine are such worlds apart from Granny's.

CHAPTER THREE

ALFRED AND EDITH

During the 1950s Granny used to take me for holidays to her close friend, Marion Wallwork's chalet in Dinas Bay, Anglesey – I presume to get me out from under Mum's feet. As soon as we reached the Menai Bridge we'd sing and I was allowed a Fox's Glacier Mint, which Granny kept

Alfred off to War - 1914

secreted in the glove compartment of her black Morris Minor. It was a great adventure for me. She was a purposeful woman and I was always slightly fearful of her.

Edith with Joan, David & Kay – 1919

My Grandmother, Edith Elise Hickling, was born on 16th January, 1889. I found scant details of her childhood but gathered it was formal, shaping her into a dignified and determined woman. I wonder if she visited her uncle in France? I often regret not asking more about her early life and if she had much to do with her uncle Fred. Granny married Alfred Wyatt Smith at the Parish Church of St. Giles, Northampton on 5th November, 1914. Connected to many charities, she became known to her friends as

Mrs W.V.S Smith because of her long and devoted service during the war to the Women's Voluntary Service (later the WRVS), and like her grandfather Julius she was a member of the Hallé Concerts Society in Manchester. For all her sterling charity works, in 1955 Edith was awarded the MBE in the Birthday Honours List. She worked tirelessly for so many worthy causes but I only knew the family side of her life.

I never met my grandfather, Alfred Wyatt Smith. No one spoke much about him but later I discovered snippets of his life. Born 10th September 1891, he served throughout World War One as Captain of the 6th Cheshire Regiment and in the Intelligence Corps. During World War Two he was commissioned with the Royal Air Force, and owing to military postings he and Granny moved around, living in rooms. When the war ended, he went into his father's cotton business, Tootal, Broadhurst of Oxford Road, Manchester, and eventually became a director. (This explains all the rolls of cotton fabric Mum used for making curtains and dresses.) He was responsible for the building of the Ryecroft Home for the Church of England Children's Society at Worsley. Their first-born was Edith Joan on 9th February, 1916, followed closely by Irene Kathleen Rosemary, Mum, born on 3rd May, 1917 in Oban House, Pensarn, Wales.

In 1918, with Alfred established in his trade and financially secure, Alfred and Edith moved into their first real home – Meadow Bank, Worsley, Manchester. It was an idyllic place to raise their family. Auntie Joan told me, 'It was a grand old long house with nine bedrooms. There were various staff, one cook, two gardeners, two housemaids, a nanny and a chauffeur. There were always dogs running around the house, birds with broken wings and injured wild animals in boxes Kay had rescued.'

My Grandmother, Edith Elise Smith

Three sons soon followed: Alfred David Raymond on 8th July, 1919, then Michael on 15th December, 1921 and John Berwick on 10th September, 1923. Their family complete, Alfred and Edith commissioned Thomas Cantrell Dugdale to paint a portrait of the children with their nanny in their sitting room. Auntie Joan said he visited Meadow Bank several times for sittings and became known as 'Uncle Duggie'. He lived in London and was a member of the Royal Academy and the Royal Portrait Society, painting many important portraits and scenes from World War One.

Michael, Kay, David, Joan, Berwick with nanny at Meadow Bank. 1923. Painted by Thomas Cantrell Dugdale RA

Mum spoke very little of her father, perhaps because she rarely saw him, and also because she hated his favourite hobby – golf. He sounded quite a character. Once on the Worsley golf links he entered the 'longest drive' dressed as a woman and won! He was a scratch golfer and Captain of the Royal Lytham Club in 1935, and in that year he presented the American professional, Lawson Little, with a winning trophy. Alfred was nicknamed 'Smiter' because he was a champion of long shots and could beat anyone.

Alfred at the Royal Lytham Club presenting Lawson Little with the winning trophy, 1935

He spent many weekends at the Club golfing, drinking and playing cards. It was here he met his future son-in-law, Jos. I can imagine them driving back to Worsley together on Sunday nights chatting about their best shots and latest business strategies. I believe Alfred also regularly visited the Windermere Golf Club, driving up to the Lakes for weekends and calling at the Eagle and Child in Staveley en route.

Alfred and Edith on the lawn at Meadow Bank, 1934

CHAPTER FOUR

SCHOOL DAYS

Whenever I asked Mum about her school days she would just say, 'Oh, that was too long ago to remember.' But Auntie Joan was able to tell me that Kro's Nest, a walk from their house in Worsley, was her first school, where Mrs Milnes was head teacher. At thirteen, as was the family tradition, Mum and Joan were packed off to St. Leonards boarding school in St. Andrews, Scotland. Both her Mother and Great Aunt Mary (Alfred's sister) had previously attended, believing that this was the right school to prepare girls for '*life*'. Joan was in Abbey Park House and Mum went into St. Nicholas. Aged only one year apart, they travelled together by train from Manchester to Scotland at the beginning and end of each term, but at school their paths never crossed.

The hockey team at St Leonards School, 1932. Kay - third from left

Mum hated lacrosse, hockey and domestic science: she was musical and loved learning the piano and 'cello. She once told me that during the carriage journey from the train station to school, her 'cello fell off and smashed irreparably. Perhaps that's why, years later, she was so keen to buy me a 'cello. An ex-school chum, Joan Whitworth, who later lived nearby in Skelwith Bridge, remembered how sensitive and musical Mum was. Whilst looking through a rather battered brown album, I found many of her school photos taken at St. Leonards and at her final school.

During 1933-34 Mum attended the most expensive girls' finishing school in Switzerland – Collège Alpin Beau Soleil. She once told me that she had a lot of fun on the ski slopes with her new friends. I wondered if she walked around with a book on her head to improve deportment? If so, it worked! Mum had a very stylish stride.

Kay on the balcony
College Alpin Beau Soleil, 1934

My secondary school art teacher, Mary Burkett, once told me that she could recognise Kay from a distance because of the way she walked. Joan, who was a year ahead at Beau Soleil, remembers: 'It was fun – house monitors were in charge, they were royalty. We took more notice of them than the teachers and we had complete freedom.'

Summer holidays were spent with the family at St. Annes-on-Sea, at Criccieth, North Wales, or with Granny and Grandpa Smith in Prestbury, Cheshire, or Granny and Grandpa Hickling in Nottingham.

Skiing College Alpin Beau Soleil, 1934. Kay 2nd from left

On one occasion when Mum's father drove her home from Switzerland via Paris, he bought her a new hat. 'I was terribly thrilled,' she recalled. However, her father wasn't terribly thrilled by what followed. On leaving school in 1934, Mum was given the choice of studying music in Vienna or training at the Royal Academy of Dramatic Art. She chose the latter – to which her father responded, 'Oh dear, head in the clouds!'

11

Patrick and Judith have gone home. I've returned to Rosewood alone to feed and cuddle Bob. As he's a stray, I don't know exactly how old he is, but I can see he's pining and desperate for some love. The cats, Jester and Snowdrop, are still in much need of attention. I've already taken Snowdrop to the vets where they treated him for malnutrition. I just pray he will improve.

I drive on to see Mum, via Hawkshead and Esthwaite Lake to Haverthwaite. She's smiling today and looks well. This makes me happy. I know she's getting the warmth and care she needs. While we're chatting away I record her talking about the past. As soon as I place the microphone on the table in front of her, she sits up straight and composes herself as if to deliver the stage performance of her life. She's enjoying our memory sessions and I'm learning so much more about her, even though sometimes she needs a little prompting. I'm realising how our lives differ, how privileged she was. I ask about her acting days. She might suspect I've been rooting through her drawers at home so I decide not to tell her that inside an old worn leather folder I've found some old newspaper clippings — theatre reviews.

Chapter Five

HER CHOICE

Mum registered at the Royal Academy of Dramatic Art on 10th September, 1935 and loved it; the parties, champagne (her favourite drink), oyster silk ball gowns, high heels and her many boyfriends, one of whom was Jon Pertwee, who left RADA after refusing to play a 'West Wind'. He went on to have a long and successful acting career, including two well-known television characters, 'Worzel Gummidge' and 'Doctor Who'. Peter Williams, another handsome beau, also became a successful actor, appearing in the intriguing wartime story called *The Man Who Never Was*.

Kay Delius RADA, 1937

Michael Callan - the actor, 1937

Mum excelled in her studies and on 13th January, 1937, registered her stage name as Kay Delius. A year later, on 25th January, she left RADA to join the Barry O'Brien repertory company alongside Kenneth More and Anthony Marlowe. The summer of 1939 was spent touring England and during that time she met her future husband: my father Dan Callaghan, whose stage name was Michael Callan.

They performed in such plays as *Housemaster* by Ian Hay at the Coliseum Theatre, London, Mum playing 'Ellen' and Dad, 'Victor Beamish'. Other plays included *Poison Pen* at the Garrick Theatre, the Exeter Theatre and the Lyceum, where 'There was a very bright and enjoyable lovers' quarrel by Miss Kay Delius and Michael Callan, playing Malcolm McLeod and Rose Rainrider.' *The Amazing Dr. Clitterhouse* was staged at Eastbourne, the Wood Green Empire and the Chiswick Empire where, at an evening for Ivor Novello, the star himself arrived unexpectedly to inaugurate a nine-week season of plays at the theatre. In a speech he said, 'Kinema, wireless and television had all done their best to kill theatre, but had not succeeded, I do not think that it ever will.' How right he was! In this play Mum took the part of 'a charming nurse Anne. Michael Callan, Lorraine Clewes, John Dunkley and Jack Denton form a formidable gang as Green, Daisy, Wilson and Lee respectively.'

Cartoonist's impressions - 'Poison Pen' at the Garrick Theatre

On the few occasions I took Mum to London, whenever we travelled on the Tube, the moment she spotted Goodge Street, she'd say, with a faraway look in her eyes, 'This is where I got off to go to RADA to rehearse.'

Mum and Dad made a stage pact vowing only to perform in plays together, but this didn't last. Dad played Paul Evans in *The Girl Who Couldn't*

Programme & Ivor Novello's appearance at Chiswick Theatre 1939

Quite at the Intimate Theatre, Palmers Green, London as well as at the Bristol Old Vic and The Theatre Royal, King Street, Bristol, and in 1938 played the part of Peter Pearson in *Quiet is Best* by John Clements, who ran the Intimate Theatre.

Ten years later, my brother Patrick remembered, 'I was taken to a pantomime in which Dad was performing in London. We met up with a fellow actor who could remove the top of his thumb and replace it and contort his neck in a peculiar way.' This was *Treasure Island* at the Piccadilly Theatre in 1948, where Dad played 'Deadeye'. Patrick was seven years old. My sister Judith, who was four years old and also in the audience, added, 'I had a hard time reconciling the idea that the pirate we were talking to was Dad. It was only when he wiped away his makeup I realised who he was.'

CHAPTER SIX

DAD

In my eyes Dad could do no wrong. Perhaps because he was a rarity, hardly at home; and when he was, he treated me kindly. I thought he was gentle and mysterious. Sometimes he cooked meals for me in the middle of the night when everyone else was asleep, and he always stood up for me if I'd been a bit naughty. I couldn't understand why Mum hardly ever talked about him and, when she did, her face and whole body stiffened. He was stocky, strong and ten years older than Mum, and had packed quite a bit more into his life at sea, his stage career and later in London on civvy street. Perhaps he was quite wild in his youth. I remember him mentioning his drinking chums, Lawrence Olivier and Jack Hawkins, amongst other actors, who were carving out their careers during the 1940's. He had two aunts, his father's sisters Noel and Stella and when, in 1925, his parents left him behind, I believe he lived with one of them in Chelsea when he wasn't away at naval college.

Dan - Royal Naval College, 1920

Many years later, in 1964, I stayed with him in his flat at Blackheath. It was my first experience of London and very strong coffee. One morning we were walking back to his flat on Shooters Hill when he stopped to talk to a man. He was rather strange, I thought, because his voice was deep and croaky. I noticed he wore a cravat like Dad, but each time he spoke, he pressed his throat. Dad introduced me to him: 'My darling this is Jack.' It didn't dawn on me until years later that it was Jack Hawkins. At the time he was suffering from throat cancer and had to speak through a mechanical larynx. Like Dad, he was a 'three-pack-a-day' smoker.

I traced Dad's family back to Cahir O'Callaghan (born 1596) of Dromaneen Castle, Co. Cork, Ireland. This was one of the three main castles of the ancient O'Callaghan clan: Dromore and Clonmeen being the others. After four generations, in 1758, the 'O' preceding Callaghan was dropped. Dad's grandfather, Sir George Astley Callaghan (1852-1920), served as Britain's commander-in-chief of the Home Fleet as World War One approached. He was highly regarded until, much to everyone's shock and embarrassment, Sir Winston Churchill, the First Sea Lord, replaced him with George's deputy – Admiral Jellico.

Sir George Astley Callaghan Admiral of the Fleet

Dad was born on 5th January, 1907 at Devonport (formerly Stoke Damerel), Devon, the eldest son of Cyril (Commander in Chief, Naval Home Command) and Dorothy Callaghan. He had two sisters, Biddy and Patsy, and two brothers, Barry and Michael. It seemed he was destined for a career at sea. Firstly he joined the Royal Naval College, Osborne, Isle of Wight, which was in the process of being closed down, then in January

Biddy, Dan and Patsy Callaghan

1922 he moved to Dartmouth as a member of the fifth term. After several re-takes, he passed out in May, 1924.

His parents lived at a house called Nansladron in Cornwall. It had beautiful gardens and several acres of land, but sadly, this family home was not to remain theirs. On a gentleman's handshake during a round of golf one day, his father sold Nansladron and moved to South Africa with the promise of a thriving business. Auntie Biddy told me, 'Our last five years were spent in Cornwall, before coming to South Africa in 1925, when Daddy got in tow with a couple of South Africans, supposedly to go farming together; but when Daddy arrived they said the farm was too small for partners and he had to try and find somewhere else for us to go. Mummy and four of us were arriving on the same ship, due for its 2nd voyage. What an upheaval that was!'

Consequently Dad was left to fend for himself in England. He must have missed his family and roots because he apparently paid them a visit. In a letter dated 26th February, 1930 from the White Star Line, from Australia, I found this report:

For the particular voyage in question, a stowaway – Dan Callaghan – was taken on to London at the Board of Trade request, and landed there. With this exception, all other passengers by the vessel in the usual course were disembarked at Southampton ... much regretting the delay caused.

By all accounts Dad spent his 21st birthday in South Africa, and in order to return to England without money, did the obvious thing. Mum once told me, 'He never settled, always wanted to be somewhere else.'

* * *

At last, a beautiful sunny day. The River Brathay is sparkling and birds are singing but travelling over here from Kendal to Skelwith, sometimes twice a day, is beginning to wear me down emotionally and physically. Judith's daughter Emma has taken the youngest cat, Jester, home to Guildford, Surrey, and I've decided to take old Bob back home. He's a big heavy boy but I manage to heave him into the back of our car. He hates car travel and is very wobbly and sick. Once home, Steve and I bed him down in the warm kitchen, where he drinks copious amounts of water. By the morning he's peed everywhere but we don't mind, just clean up and take him through our garden to familiarise him with his new home. I telephone Mum and assure her that he's safe with us, but I feel sorry that he's too unsteady to take to see her at Hollow Oak.

Even though I'm satisfied Mum is now safe, I'm so aware that our world has changed. I try to imagine how Mum coped in the past with circumstances beyond her control.

Chapter Seven

THEIR WAR YEARS

On September 2nd, 1939 at 11.15 a.m. BST, the Prime Minister, Neville Chamberlain, announced that the final British ultimatum for the withdrawal of German troops from Poland had expired at 11a.m., and that 'consequently this country is at war with Germany.'

Dan & Kay on their wedding day
Grimsby 12ᵗʰ Oct 1939

Mum and Dad had just completed their first touring season together when theatres began to close down, and as a result they were out of work. Dad was preparing to go off to war when, on 12th October, 1939, they married in Grimsby, Dad already in uniform. Naval postings took him all over England, which must have made a difficult start to their marriage, as Mum soon discovered.

Their first home was Cherry Tree Cottage, Gorran Haven, Cornwall – a little white bungalow near the sea where they took in their first cat Topsy and Spaniel dog Janie. Then in 1940 they moved to Park Cottage, Gorran Haven. That first summer appears to have been happy. From the photos I found, Dad worked on his kitchen garden, theatre friends came to stay, and they enjoyed picnics on Gorran Haven beach.

Dad's next posting was to Haverfordwest, Wales, where on 24th September 1941 my brother Patrick was born. Very soon afterwards they were transferred to Ramsgate. Mum remembered, 'I had to drive to Kent by car with my baby. As it grew dark it was difficult to see as my headlights were reduced to slits so as not to be seen from above. I wasn't quite sure where I was going, there were no signposts, so I had to rely on an old map and asking people on the way. I finally arrived and found the house was perched on the cliff tops looking out to sea. It was strange and dark and difficult to find a room for us to sleep in. Little did I know that this house served as the early warning air raid station. Time after time Patrick woke up screaming.'

This is something I never experienced, but Patrick remembers watching the formations of German bombers filling the sky, under attack from the anti-aircraft defences. Mum said she used to take chances walking Patrick along the beach in a pram and sometimes saw the bombers flying beneath the radar above the English Channel. On one occasion she rushed to get Patrick down some steps into a cave but panicked because she couldn't release the halter fasteners and ended up pushing the whole pram with baby down the steps. Times were difficult surviving on that cliff top, with Dad away at war and the constant fear for Patrick's safety. When Dad was posted to the Orkneys, Mum didn't follow; instead she returned to her Mother and Father at Worsley, near Manchester.

Granny Callaghan in South Africa must have felt for her daughter-in-law so far away, because Auntie Joan told me, 'Throughout the war food hampers from South Africa arrived regularly for Kay, especially at Christmas'.

Janie

Kay, Gorran Haven

Kay & Dan Gorran Haven beach 1939/40

Kay & Dan move to Park Cottage Cornwall, 1940

21

CHAPTER EIGHT

LOST LOVE

Dad and his brother, Lt. George Barry Callaghan, who had returned from South Africa to serve in the Royal Air Force, often spent their leaves together at Meadow Bank. It must have been a luxury for them to stay in that house – comfortable and everything taken care of.

One early May weekend, Dad's leave was cancelled so Barry travelled to Worsley alone. In that short insecure time, when normal companionship was rare, Mum and Barry spent the evenings together talking and walking in the garden. Barry was stationed at Wick, Scotland, as part of Coastal Command. On the night of 23rd May 1942, whilst on active duty with 608 Squadron, after signalling a successful attack on an enemy vessel, he was listed missing over the North Sea. His body was washed ashore at Kinn Island, near Trondheim, Norway. Barry was twenty-eight years old, leaving his wife Dawn and two young sons, Anthony and Christopher, in South Africa. Whenever I asked Mum about Barry, she fell silent and refused to talk any more about him. I will never know if Dad was aware that his brother had spent that leave alone with Mum.

Barry, August 1931

On February 27th 1944 my sister Judith Anne was born at Patricroft Hospital, Eccles. Her first memory was of meeting her father: 'I remember being in Mum's arms at a railway station where a train had just pulled in and steam was belching out onto the platform. As people were disembarking and walking along through the steam, my attention was directed to a man in uniform coming towards us. He was smiling, and amid hugs etc. I was told he was my Dad. I had never seen him until then as he had been away in the Navy serving off the coast of Crete in Air Sea Rescue.'

While Mum, Patrick and Judith continued to live in the relative safety of Meadow Bank, she received a letter dated 24th July 1944 from her brother David – Captain A.D.R. Smith, who was serving with the Second Battalion, Royal Warwickshire Regiment, B.L.A. Letters were precious – it read, 'I'm OK, bombs dropping outside, strange faces popping in and out, some just stay out, they don't bother to bring 'em in – it's all so fantastic this war; a series of extraordinary noises and smells! May sound funny, but that's about all it amounts to, one can describe most things that way…' 'B.L.A.' was the British Liberation Army – the British sector of the force sent to liberate France in the D-Day Landings. So David played his part in the liberation of Europe; but sadly this was his last letter; for shortly afterwards he too was killed.

How difficult those times must have been for so many; losing sons and brothers, with bombing, rationing, and the separation of husbands and wives. I doubt I will ever experience this kind of hardship but I do remember the sorrow Mum went through on Remembrance Sunday and anniversaries of David and Barry's deaths.

* * *

Even after administering vitamins, having his nails cut, etc., sadly this morning I find Snowdrop dead at the bottom of the airing cupboard. I bury him in the garden and decide not to tell Mum about him just yet. Bob is also deteriorating. His irrational behaviour worries me. He walks around in circles as if his brain is malfunctioning. What can I do to help him?

CHAPTER NINE

No. 3 PRIORY WAY, LONDON

When the war ended in 1945, Mum, Dad, Patrick, Judith, their dog Janie and cat Topsy left Manchester to settle in London. Their new home – No 3 Priory Way, Headstone Lane, Pinner – was a 1930s semi-detached house with a long narrow garden stretching behind. Dad and Mum appeared to enjoy building their new life together growing flowers and vegetables as every household did along that row. Family life was sweet and smooth for the first time.

But just as normality was resuming, in January 1948, Mum's father died. It must have been sudden and a great shock to her as he was only fifty-seven years old. Later that year on July 24th I was born in Pinner. Then more changes followed. Her mother sold the family home, Meadow Bank, and on September 5th 1949 moved into a more manageable house, No 2 Woodstock Drive, Worsley. I imagine this must have been unsettling for Mum. Fortunately she had a good neighbour, Phyllis Smith, who became a lifelong friend and my Godmother. She

Dan, Judith, Kay & Patrick, 1947

Janie at No3 Priory Way

Leaving Meadow Bank - Sept 5th 1949

worked at London University, looked after her mother and never married. I was very fond of her. She was a precise woman, impeccably dressed in calf-length pleated skirts, and always sported a neat silk scarf. Etiquette was of the utmost importance.

If she felt things weren't quite up to scratch she would say, 'Coo, Mrs C., that's awfully non-U!' in an exaggerated posh cockney accent! Her quaintness and sense of humour were charming, almost fussy, but she cared deeply for Mum and her family.

Mum's brother Berwick, who was a photographer at the time, came to live with them. They got on well and he took many black and white photos of us children. He entered a photo of Judith into the Vinolia Soap Makers Competition, and on 21st October 1949 Mum received a letter to say she'd won a prize – a Mason Pearson hairbrush.

Patrick and Judith went to the local school (St Andrew's, North Harrow) but Judith had continuing health problems. At a few months old she contracted whooping cough, which at that time was a killer. Two years later she was in Great Ormond Street Hospital having an operation on her trigger thumbs, and a tonsillectomy. This is when Mum discovered Judith's 'funnel chest', which meant her chest

Patrick, Kay, Judith & Kerry
No.3 Priory Way, 1949

was concave and she sometimes found breathing difficult. Mum thought it had been bought on by lying in bed so nothing was done until later. (I now realise why Mum made a fuss and worried over Judith particularly in the cold damp weather.)

Judith's dolls house

Judith & Patrick, Kerry's christening 1949

Little baker ~ Judith, Nov 1948

Kerry & Kay ~ christening day
Sunday 15th May, 1949

Kerry on the lawn at Priory Way

Dad managed to find more acting work, playing the part of Deadeye again in *Treasure Island* at the Fortune Theatre, but like so many men after the war he returned home a changed man. After serving in Air Sea Rescue, hauling out the drowned off Crete night after night, he was tormented, restless, and began drinking. I believe he spent some time in a rehabilitation home but I'm not sure where. The awful effects of the war formed the first holes in my parents' marriage, which was sinking fast. Mum, desperate to escape him and London, was at a crossroads.

* * *

Today I spend the day at Hollow Oak and record our conversations. Some days Mum's recall is sharp but other times woolly. Today the nurses tell me she's lacking vitamin B12 and they have to inject her, which she loathes as it hurts and bruises her arm badly. I notice she's walking much more slowly now and holds onto the handrail in the corridor. I'm getting quite concerned. I decide not to tell her about Snowdrop and I hide the truth about Bob. Two nights ago he had worsened and we had to make the decision to take him to the vets. I won't forget that icy night, sky full of stars. The outcome was heartbreaking for us but kinder for Bob. I feel so responsible and guilty. I want to remember happier times, know more about hers. Mum is sitting up and waiting for me to switch on the recorder

'Mum, what do you remember about arriving in the North?'

• PART TWO •

CHAPTER TEN

ARRIVING IN PARADISE

Mum smiles: 'I was thrilled to bits. Peace at last, although I got a shock on the first morning when I woke to the sound of the wood yard on one side and the stone mill on the other side of the river. I wondered what on earth all the noise was. I soon got used to it – after all, it was someone's living and part of this community.'

It was Auntie Joan who told me how Mum found Rosewood. Joan's sister-in-law Nin – the sister of Joan's husband Jos – owned a small wooden chalet tucked into the hillside at Finsthwaite in the Lake District. They called it 'The Hut'. Jos, Joan and their children spent many happy holidays there.

One day, as Nin was driving through the quiet village of Skelwith Bridge, she saw a 'For Sale' notice outside a wooden bungalow by the River Brathay and thought this would be just the ticket for Kay. Granny and Mum drove up from Worsley to view the property. Nin was right: without a second breath, Mum fell in love with this 'little shack by the river', as she often called it. It was on the market for £1,900; and with some financial help from her brother-in-law Jos and her mother she bought her new home.

Mrs Ridyard and her daughter Nancy were living there at the time, but as Nancy had met and married John Carpenter, who worked across the road at the Greenbank timber yard, they'd decided to return to John's home town, Nottingham. Nancy was an expert climber, setting up many new routes with her friends Mabel Barker and Tony Musgrave during the 1930's. Mum must have related to this, imagining her own new-found freedom walking the fells. On 12th June 1950 she moved into 'The Bungalow' and renamed it 'Rosewood'.

Whilst Mum was busy buying and moving into Rosewood, she shipped Judith and Patrick off to Uncle Jos and Auntie Joan's in Freckleton, Preston, and, as I was only a baby, I remained with Mum. Judith remembers the day she arrived at Skelwith with Auntie Joan and family. Thinking she would be returning with them to Freckleton, she couldn't believe it when she spotted Mum across the road leaning over a garden gate waving and smiling.

CHAPTER ELEVEN

LIKE AN ARK

Built on a site that had once held the old gunpowder works and store serving the Langdale quarries in the 19th century, Rosewood was wooden throughout – made of two 1917 army huts joined together and raised on mortared stone foundations. It stood in 'one Rood 38 perches' according to the old deeds – almost one acre. The River Brathay flowed past the north side – sometimes like a lion, and sometimes a lamb. It was our playground where we stone-raced, found fossils, swam in Adam's Dub – and many a time, nearly drowned! The Coniston to Ambleside road bordered the south side, with only few cars and the occasional charabanc. The house was long and low – stretched out as if lulled to sleep by the music of the river; but it was about to be woken!

The exterior bleached-green paint was peeling. The felt roof had split and leaked in several places. It made a thunderous sound when it rained, and with no insulation summers were hot and in winters it was so cold we could scrape early morning frost-ferns off the inside of the windows.

Rosewood ~ back garden

I'm not sure if Dad intended moving north or if Mum wanted him to but he soon followed her. Perhaps she thought he would overcome his heavy drinking and make a new start.

I remember him calling Mum 'Kitty' or 'Kate' and for some reason this made me feel safe even though at times I detected a frosty atmosphere between them. Perhaps he was making a huge effort to change his ways and things would work out between them. It appeared their new life began to dance. They got stuck into the refurbishments, though with very little money it was a slow process. New linoleum, carpets, a bath, bedding and, of course, gallons of paint purchased from 'Tinny Martins' in Ambleside. I still love the smell of paint.

The interior tongue-and-groove boarding, layered with various dismal shades of brown gloss, was soon transformed into pastel yellows and blues reflecting the sunlight pouring up the valley. Small-paned windows, too high for us to reach, opened inwards and were held by a bracket – just enough to let in a cool breeze on a summer's day. The sparsely furnished rooms echoed. A narrow hall opened into a large sitting room into which, as well as a table, chairs and sofa, Mum placed her upright piano. I remember we had a brown table-top Bush radio with only two dials, which was soon replaced by a luxurious highly-polished radiogram. It had a turntable on which Mum played her Frank Sinatra and classical records. It seemed to be a precious thing and we were forbidden to touch it in case we scratched the records or broke

needles. We listened to *Arthur Askey, Housewives' Choice, Mrs Dale's Diary*, and on Sundays *The Billy Cotton Band Show*, and although I found it boring and didn't understand the jokes, there was much laughter during *The Navy Lark*.

A green tiled fireplace with a back boiler was the only form of heating, and above that hung a stag's head – not Mum's idea of décor, but nevertheless it was a talking point. The game was to throw hats at the antlers. Beyond was a simple galley kitchen with an old gas stove on legs and basic wooden cupboards. I remember the baking cupboard, with frosted glass and a surface that opened out for rolling pastry. To keep the flies

Looking towards Wansfell from lower garden, 1950's

at bay, we had a meat safe instead of a fridge. Milk soured and many a plate of mouldy food had to be thrown away. Mum washed up at an earthenware sink under a window overlooking a terrace and the river, alive with dippers, kingfishers and herons. There was one cold tap fixed to a lead pipe and water had to be pumped up from a well in the garden. When the tank in the loft ran dry, as it often did, Mum would shout to whoever was in the bathroom next door to turn on the pump. There followed a roaring noise for the next half an hour while water spluttered into the tank in the loft. No-one considered the danger of an electric plug in the bathroom. The pump in the cellar always froze in winter and had to be defrosted with boiling water. On those days we scampered down to the river to break the ice and collect water for washing, shivering and shrieking, our breath like smoke.

Next to the kitchen was the 'little room' – the hub of the house, where we ate our meals, played games and dressed for school around the cherry-red tiled fireplace, each of us pushing and shoving to get closest to the heat.

Patrick became a magician in this room, performing his tricks, while Judith and I became actresses, presenting our own plays much to the amusement of Aunts and Granny. At the other end of the house were four good-sized bedrooms, one reserved for visitors. As the bathroom was too far to find in the middle of the night, we used potties. Everywhere smelled of damp, paraffin, lights (cheap dog food) simmering on the stove, and Patrick's chemistry. He spent hours experimenting in his bedroom, heating chemicals on a Bunsen burner into some awful explosive substance. He was keen on science, enthusiastic about Patrick Moore, and a huge fan of *Journey into Space* – though as soon as its opening bars

Patrick the magician!

played on the radio, I raced along to the bedroom and hid. It made Mum laugh, probably with relief that I had actually hopped off to bed. My joy was reading *Heidi*, or Lassie books – and my favourite, *The Snow Goose* by Paul Gallico. I remember Mum reading this story at bedtime to Judith and me until we sobbed into our pillows.

Kerry & Judith

Apart from a few pines, clipped box and azaleas, the garden was wild and open. Granny helped pay for a small local firm called Hayes to re-design and lay out the front garden with rockeries, rhododendrons, hydrangeas – acid-loving plants which suited the soil. In Spring their perfume filled the air, and fallen petals looked like miniature skirts we loaded onto sticks. It gave us hours of fun. We used to run along the slate paths, hide in box hedges finding bird and bees nests, and even though

Dad would mysteriously disappear then re-appear, he maintained the garden beautifully. He planted formal flower-beds with spring bulbs, wallflowers, pansies and antirrhinums (snapdragons) which I squeezed to make them talk. Patrick warned me not to touch the red hot pokers as they were 'red hot!' Behind the house he created a

Kay on steps ~ Kerry, Patrick & Judith in the garden, 1955

productive kitchen garden with apple trees, vegetables and herbs, gooseberries, red and blackcurrants. We were paid a penny a pound to pick and top'n'tail the fruit for Mum to make into jams and jellies. In the summer her kitchen steamed with dripping jelly bags and rows of red jars. Our clothes airing on the Sheila Maid reeked of jam or bacon. Alongside the kitchen garden, Dad kept a few hens in a wooden ark. I remember putting my hand through the side door flaps and feeling the straw for warm eggs. I was told always to leave one for the hens to lay to. Mum loved Rosewood and told me, 'It had a natural look and sound about it.' But hidden amongst this beauty were some harsh realities.

Kay with Kim on the top lawn

Patrick, Judith, Kay, Kerry & Sheila above Elterwater

Chapter Twelve

SURVIVING

After the initial excitement of purchasing and moving into Rosewood, money had to be found to pay the bills. Tourists had been visiting the Lake District since Victorian times, and apart from the Skelwith Bridge Hotel, there were no cafés or bed and breakfast accommodation in the village. Mum seized the opportunity. She rolled up her sleeves and put a sign on the gate: 'Bed and Breakfast 12/6d. a night including Evening Meal.' I remember her dinners were simple but nutritious, mainly consisting of braised beef or lamb and two veg. She opened a tea garden and turned the little room into a shop selling sweets. I remember the boxes of Rolos, Smarties, Bounty and Mars Bars, Wagon Wheels and Kendal Mint Cake, which we were allowed to stack on a counter for sale. She also sold fizzy drinks. Dandelion and burdock, lemonade and Vimto were favourites. They were supplied by Morecambe and Direct Supplies and arrived in wooden crates. A penny was given to anyone returning an empty bottle (which most customers did). She installed a large freezer, and a local firm called Eldorado supplied ice cream in oblong blocks, delivered in a large wooden swill. (Swills were a traditional South Lakeland oval basket crafted from oak or hazel and used for carrying seeds, root

crops, laundry etc… and in this case, ice cream!) The blocks were cut into even portions and served to customers in wafers – vanilla, chocolate… Strawberry and pineapple were my favourite.

Tea by the river ~ Jess waiting patiently for crumbs

Across the road at Greenbank lived a six-year-old girl called Sheila Bamforth who, curious to know who had moved in next door, discovered it was a girl her own age. Sheila told me that before Judith had even entered the door at Rosewood, she marched up to her and announced: 'Hello, I'm Judith and I've come to play.' From then on they were best friends and couldn't be separated – in each other's houses all the time.

I made friends with Pippa Manby, who lived at Mill Brow farm, half a mile from Rosewood. I could signal Pippa from our shop window. We'd play Cowboys and Indians out in the backs of Mill Brow all day, mimicking *The Lone Ranger*, which we were allowed to watch on her television. We didn't have one.

There was little choice regarding schooling. Patrick attended the local St Mary's Primary School in Ambleside, then moved on as a weekly boarder to The Craig in Windermere. Judith also attended Ambleside School, then The Old College, Windermere and finally Hawkshead School. After failing my eleven plus examination, I went from Ambleside to Hawkshead School until the John Ruskin Secondary Modern in Coniston opened in 1960.

* * *

Today is October 12th, Mum's wedding anniversary. Will she remember? I don't have time to take her out – besides, it's blowing a gale and raining hard, so we stay in the warmth of her room and chat over cups of coffee. She's very pleased to hear that her cat Jester has settled at Emma's, but sadly I'll have to tell her about Bob soon. A man pops his head around Mum's door and starts singing 'I wonder who's kissing her now?' He has a Scottish accent, a ruddy complexion and pale red hair. He looks very dapper in shirt and tie. At the end of his charming rendition he smiles and disappears. After he's gone I look at Mum as if to say, who is that?

'Oh, that's Bill, we sometimes have lunch together and he's always singing to me but I take no notice.' Judging by her dancing blue-grey eyes, I suspect she likes being serenaded. I'm pleased to see she's joining the residents in the dining room and making friends, especially Bill. Mum sits quietly for a moment as if contemplating something. She looks up at me and asks, 'When am I going home?' I promise that when she's better – next week, I will take her home for a visit.

I hand her an old photo. 'When was this taken? And who is the man standing on the left?' Mum smiles and peers into the faded black and white scene of four children on the steps and a man standing in the garden at Rosewood.

'That's Jim on the lawn and Patrick, Judith, Sheila and you on the steps in 1952. Do you remember?' It suddenly floods back to me how scary and high I thought those steps were, especially after my illness. And yes, of course, it's Jim Phelan, I remember him clearly now.

CHAPTER THIRTEEN

VAGABONDS

In the summer of 1952 there was a knock on the front door. When Mum went to see who it was, I followed, clinging tight to the folds of her floral linen skirt. I remember this well because of the unusual couple standing on the porch step – a young woman with long dark hair and flowing skirt, and a tall man. He appeared mysterious, like an ancient hawthorn surrounded by gypsy folk-lore. His complexion was craggy, which possibly aged him, and from under a worn hat, white hair straggled his neck. His clothes were tattered, like an autumn countryside. He spoke with a southern Irish accent which made me smile, it sounded warm and familiar: 'Me name's Jim and this is Katleen. I'll be wonderin' if you have a bite for us te eat? We' been travellin' days and this seemed a most lovely place to stop and yer have a kindly face, you do so.' And in they came.

Jim Phelan, born in 1895, was involved in the Irish Revolutionary movement and had been jailed for a murder that took place during a robbery in a sub post office in Ireland. On the eve of his execution in 1923, the Home Secretary commuted his sentence to life imprisonment (in Maidstone and Dartmoor) and he remained there until his release in 1937. He vowed he would never live permanently between four walls again, so thereafter lived the life of a vagabond. He'd met Kathleen (Newton), also known as Kay, in Garstang, England whilst hitching a lift. She, slight, young and pretty, was heading the other way. He crossed the road, they chatted for a while and then he announced: 'I've no house, no possessions, I've been a hobo in America and a swagman in Australia and the only time I had any money was when I wrote a book or a short story and sold it.' I discovered later in one of Kay's pamphlets that she responded: 'It blew my mind. It took me a couple of minutes to realise that an Irish tramp-writer from Tipperary was what I had been waiting around for. We turned westerly and went hitch-hiking together for many years until he died.'

Jim was a big man and at first I was scared, but he was also gentle and encouraged us all in our artistic and writing pursuits. He was an accomplished author, drawing on his prison life experience for his books, which included *Tramp at Anchor; Lifer; Tramping the Toby* and *Underworld*. He told us that he'd worked on scripts with Dylan Thomas, and aware that I was writing poetry and songs at the time, he sent me music and lyrics he'd written for me to sing. They returned frequently throughout the following years, selling his books and telling tales in the warmth of our fireside.

JIM PHELAN is a professional tramp. At 13 he ran away from his Dublin home to Glasgow and he has never stopped long in one place since.

He has all the same found time to be everything from blacksmith and barman to convict and revolutionary. And to write 14 books. And to marry.

His address is wherever his caravan happens to be.

This was the beginning of how Mum's life would be lived here in this quiet valley with a river running through. This was paradise, for us and for many who slept under our roof. I wanted everything to stay like this. I was unaware of Mum's personal struggles.

* * *

There's been quite a storm last night, I can hear the river raging outside and lapping the terrace. Rain has dripped in and down Mum's bedroom wall and the wallpaper is peeling. I shiver at how all the human warmth has leached from the rooms, rooms that once glowed with activity and laughter. Luckily there's enough coal left in the bunker to light another fire. I want to keep the home warm. I'm finding it a struggle to get going on the sorting today. I sit listening to the sound of cars accelerating up the hill and think about the times we used to run to the gate with great excitement to see just one car go by. We couldn't afford a car.

CHAPTER FOURTEEN

FRIENDSHIP

Each day Mum caught the bus from Skelwith to Ambleside, taking Judith to school and collecting her. Half way en route, the bus would pull in at Ashley Green to pick up Phyllis Ashton. It took no time at all for Mum and Phyllis to become good friends. They could almost have been sisters – the same good looks and sparkle. Born within a few weeks of each other and both new to the area, they

Phyllis Ashton

immediately got on as if they'd known each other for years. Phyllis also had a daughter nearly the same age as me called Kathleen.

Phyllis and her husband Geoff came from Halifax and during one cycling holiday they fell in love with the Lakes and wanted to stay. Geoff got a job working with photographic papers for Kentmere Ltd. in Staveley. He was a keen photographer and experimented with different colours and coatings which were new on the market. With their husbands working away or out all day, Mum and Phyllis spent many afternoons together. On the days Mum went off walking, Phyllis took care of me, and in turn, Kathleen often came to stay with us at Rosewood. After a while Geoff and Phyllis found it too expensive living at Ashley Green and considered returning to Halifax. With some persuasion and promotion from Kentmere Ltd., Geoff remained in his job and they moved to Gowan Cottage in Staveley. It was a large house with considerable renovation to be done. Mum helped by scrubbing floors and painting walls. Together they made curtains with fabric from Mum's brother-in-law, Jos. During this time Geoff and Phyllis spent the weekends at Rosewood. Phyllis told me, 'We'd arrive on a Friday night. We'd sit by the river, Geoff sometimes fishing and Dan bringing out glasses of sherry – he introduced me to sherry. Kay made the most wonderful fish pie and your father was such a gentleman, always made me feel completely at ease and welcome.' This was the beginning of their life-long friendship.

CHAPTER FIFTEEN

WHO IS THIS WOMAN?

When I asked Sheila what she remembered about her new neighbours – us – coming to live opposite, she told me that Skelwith villagers were shocked by this attractive newcomer in their midst who appeared to be single, had glamorous black hair and a trim figure, took in strangers, wore strappy sun-dresses, and what's more, gardened in her shorts! But Mum gradually diverted their mistrust and persuaded them otherwise. She joined the Skelwith committee, helping to organise whist drives, jumble sales, bring-and-buys with raffles and coffee mornings. The prizes were always practical: a load of logs, a goose, a hundredweight of coal, chicken dinners and Nanny Burns's fruit cake, which was very popular. The proceeds mostly went towards the children's Christmas Party and the summer village outing to Morecambe.

For months we saved our pocket money for this day trip. It seemed to be such a huge event, and a very long journey on the old roads via Windermere, Staveley, Kendal and Carnforth. We were very excited to be given a 10/- note to spend as we boarded the Ribble coach early in the morning on the corner below the Skelwith Bridge Hotel. It was a game to see who could see the sea first. After a morning of fun on Heysham sands digging sand castles and eating ice cream until we felt

Ribble coach hire from Skelwith to Morecambe, Saturday 26th June 1954

sick, we'd spend the afternoon on Morecambe promenade buying cones of cockles or shrimps. Then during our last hour or two we went to the fair. I never enjoyed this part. It was too frightening and noisy. Nevertheless, all tired and happy, we'd return in the dark singing, heads full of the fairground lights, sea and sand – topped up for another year.

Skelwith Bridge was a working, living village. There were no holiday homes then and the folk were always ready to help each other. Nanny Burns (Sheila's grandmother) and Sheila's parents Chuck and Marie Bamforth, who all lived together at Greenbank, sometimes took us in if Mum was ill or had to go away. Their house was an old whitewashed farmhouse across the road from Rosewood. They were a kind family: the fire never went out and the table was always laid with homemade teacakes, butter and jam. Mrs Eileen, who lived next door at Ivy Cottage, was another good and friendly neighbour. She kept a neat garden filled with azaleas – it was so beautiful that each spring tourists would stop and take photographs.

Harry and Bertha Mounsey lived further up the road at Craghill Cottage. Bertha was an ardent supporter of jumble sales, and we never knew why she bought so many second-hand clothes as she had no children. She'd elbow into the school trestle tables, and loaded with all manner of coats, shirts and trousers, bag them onto her bicycle to take home. We discovered later that she washed, mended and sent the clothes off to those less fortunate. Her husband Harry, who'd worked in local quarries all his life, built his and the next door house himself, and turned his hand to making wooden gates, bird tables and boxes. Mum loved to watch blue tits and nuthatches nesting in the boxes nailed to the silver birch outside her bedroom window. He also replaced all the gates at Rosewood and they lasted for years.

Mrs and Miss Swailes lived in the only other wooden bungalow up the hill. I remember they always wore gabardine trench coats and walked by with a little terrier on a lead. Everyone up the road had to walk past our house to catch the bus to Ambleside. Mr and Mrs Smithies lived at Middle Brigg Howe. They were writers, and their daughter Roberta used to come down to Rosewood once a week for piano lessons given by Mum. The Archers – mother and daughter – lived above Greenbank, and whenever they walked past our gate we thought it highly amusing to sing the theme tune from The Archers from behind the wall. We enjoyed the risk that they might be cross, but they always gave us a boiled sweet. Mum's St Leonards school friend, Joan Whitworth, lived with her mother in Spring Cottage on School Lane. I remember calling in with a present of hazelnuts picked from her own tree! Her mother was getting on in years and was lying in bed. She accepted my gift very graciously.

Across the river in the Riverside Cottages lived Edith and Stan Pepper and their daughters, Christine, Elizabeth and Susan. They also opened up a B & B and tea garden, which worried Mum at first, but ultimately there was enough trade for all. Edna and Charlie Leight lived next door. He was tall and thin, hardly spoke and used to stare at us. We were scared when we had to go and collect eggs from his hut. Mrs Fleming and Bob Williams shared the next house. Bob was

Bob Williams & Kerry on top lawn, Rosewood 1958

a fisherman and stood for hours on the banks of the river teaching me how to catch trout and perch. I envied his fine fishing rod as I had to make do with a stick, string and a bent pin that slipped the worms and maggots! (I had to supply my own bait by turning over stones in Dad's kitchen garden to find as many fat worms as possible.) Mum must have worried sometimes, especially when the river was in force, and in fact I nearly drowned twice in the torrents. The first time I was avoiding Charlie, who I thought was lurking on the bridge: I panicked and tried to cross the river, misjudging the speed of the current. I clung to a rock and managed to pull myself out breathless and very scared, realising the bridge was a better option regardless! The second time I nearly drowned was further down river. It might have been a fishing event, I'm not sure, but I leaned over the bank to look for fish and fell in out of my depth. Luckily I was hauled out and made quite a fuss of, which is perhaps why I remember it so well.

In the last house on the Riverside row lived Mr and Mrs Gray and their son Tony. I gather Mum first met them at Geoff and Phyllis Ashton's. He was a tall studious man who said very little, while she was petite, very chatty and got on well with Mum. Harry and Doris Fecitt, who owned the Kirkstone quarries, lived next to the stone mill with their three children, Harry, Elizabeth and Nicholas. The stone saw working all day was part of the music of Skelwith. They also opened a tea garden which is now 'Chesters by the River'. Roy and Judy Manby and their four children, Simon, Tim, Pippa and Linda lived at Mill Brow and although they farmed, they were also trained artists – Judy a very fine painter and Roy an architect and painter. I remember their exhibitions held in a converted barn. Judy used to make her own butter. I loved standing in the dairy watching her turn the handle of a wooden churn until the cream set to butter; nothing tasted better. Mr and Mrs Harry Wilson and their children Harry and Anne at Loughrigg Farm supplied milk for the village. Skelwith was a community that worked together to keep the village alive and Mum helped where she could, for although she wasn't religious, she played the piano when most of the village gathered for Sunday services held in the school.

The weather at Skelwith has improved and the lawns are drying out. I wish Mum was here with me to walk around the garden listening to the birdsong echoing over the river. Sadly she isn't and I can't put off all the work still to be done inside the house.

I tackle the assortment of photos, clear and wrap all the shells and fragmented china ornaments we haven't taken to Hollow Oak. All the mementos collected from beaches, holidays and grandchildren. They've been lying untouched under months of dust on Mum's old oak chest – another item bought at auction. It hasn't been opened in years and I've no idea what's inside. The rusty iron hinges creak as I lift the lid to lean against the window. It's crammed with curtains, books and more papers, and smells very musty. As I lift out the top layer I notice a creased newspaper the colour of tea. Mum kept everything to do with Royalty, especially this – The Radio Times Coronation Number, May 31st – June 6th, 1953.

Chapter Sixteen

THE CORONATION

As England prepared for the Coronation, a quote from the *Radio Times* Coronation Number (North of England Edition) read:

In the Mall, heraldic beasts climb upon four blue and gilt arches, and swinging coronets glitter beneath. Gilt trumpets lean on the summer air. Down by the river, white masts topped with plumed helmets soar above the pavements. Striped pavilions have sprung up in the parks, and the terraced stands stretch along the processional way amid a forest of waving banners. All over London, stone and brick have blossomed suddenly into a glory of rose and gold. After long months of preparation, everything is ready. The pageant is about to begin... What will be the thoughts and emotions of our young Queen as she drives to her Coronation?

Meanwhile in Skelwith Bridge, after weeks of preparation, Mr Benson's Blossom Field opposite Rosewood had been mown and pegs hammered into the ground marking starts, courses and finishing lines for different races. Everywhere you looked was red, white and blue bunting, flapping from tree to tree. Mum had prepared a makeshift awning to sell pineapple ice cream. Everyone was jubilant and ready to celebrate this grand day, June 2nd, 1953. Stan Hill, the caretaker of Skelwith School, organised the relays, egg-and-spoon race, and an obstacle race, which involved us clambering over and crawling under roped netting on the grass. There wasn't an inch of ground to stand on. All the locals stood huddled together to watch their children and friends having a good time. The fine weather held even though most were prepared for rain.

A fancy dress parade took place in the school. I remember feeling very ill and didn't want to go dressed as a rabbit. Judith wore a Hawaiian outfit. Patrick didn't enter.

Coronation Fancy Dress

Alfreda Burns	Louise Cuppage	Sheila Bamforth	Susan Park	Judith Callaghan	Carole Somerville
Elizabeth Fecitt	Kerry Callaghan	Robert Cuppage	Jaqueline Hewitson	Jean & Anne Creighton	Barry Hewitson

The Coronation tea was held in the school. Long tables overflowed with plates of sandwiches, cakes, jelly and cream – all homemade. A feast fit for not only the villagers celebrating The Crowning but almost the end of World War Two food rationing. (Tea rationing ended in 1952, rationing of sweets and sugar in 1953, and finally it all ended in 1954.)

Everyone enjoyed that day in Blossom Field. It was a happy time cherished by all, and a day Mum talked about long after.

Skelwith Coronation Sports ~ 2nd June 1953

53

CHAPTER SEVENTEEN

REALITIES

Mum taught the three of us to bear whatever knocks came our way and keep strong, but sometimes it was difficult to withstand the bullying we suffered at school and from suspicious locals who called us 'off-comers'. Was this because our accent was different? I don't know; but as Dad wasn't always there, dealing on her own with this and with three children who constantly experienced health problems, must have been a hard task for her – even though I remember not telling her about all the bullyings at school in case she thought I was to blame. I think back to how much we dared not say certain things, in case.

I often woke in the night with stomach pain. Mum would administer some bitter medicine followed by malt extract or orange juice from a small bottle, which we also had to swallow after a tablespoon of cod-liver oil. One night I remember the pain was so bad she rang for Doctor Lancaster to come quickly. It wasn't the first time he'd arrived in a coat thrown on over pyjamas, his face pale, having been sick on the path. He too may have been ill, but we guessed it was because he'd been dragged out of bed unexpectedly in the middle of the night; at least that's what he implied at the time. Anyhow, the prescribed milk of magnesia and plain food hadn't worked for me this time.

'Call Bulldog – now, an ambulance won't get here in time!' Doctor Lancaster shouted from my bedside, his hand on my pulse. (Bulldog was a taxi driver from Ambleside.)

I remember lying on the back seat of the taxi, rain on the car window turning into shiny blood-orange dots, and then blackness. Each time

I opened my eyes, flames of pain ripped through my body. I had pneumococcal peritonitis, a serious intestinal infection, and I almost died. During my recovery, Mum took me every week to have sunray treatment. I sat in a room with other children on a long bench under ultraviolet sun lamps. We had to wear goggles and I remember vividly the brightness and strong metallic smell.

Mum became a lioness nurturing and protecting us. She dealt with our health scares one after another. Her calming voice always convinced me everything would be all right. Judith suffered incessant infirmities. She told me, 'I was constantly being told to sit up straight, which I found almost impossible. Mum would take me to a clinic in the Ethel Hedley Hospital, Calgarth, Troutbeck Bridge, where it was recommended I have an exercise regime and sunray treatment. I hated this, and having to take my top off in front of all the younger boys and girls.

I was finally taken into the Royal Victoria Hospital, Blackpool, where my sternum was cut from end to end, my ribs cut off and rib cage prized open. Then they inflated my lungs for the first time. It was incredibly painful. In the coming months they collapsed several times and I remember the pain when I had to breathe hard to re-inflate them. Also during this time I was practising my ballet moves on Sheila's stone-flagged kitchen floor, and slipped. Dr. Lancaster was away and I had to wait three days, by which time I couldn't even walk. On his return, Dr Lancaster rushed me into hospital again. My leg was put in a splint and packed with gauze and cotton wool. I was told to look away while they stuck a huge needle into the bone of my leg. I was then hooked up to penicillin. It was the first time this had been used to treat osteomyelitis, which was the diagnosis.'

This, and Dad's general unpredictability, plus lack of money, must have added considerably to Mum's worries.

CHAPTER EIGHTEEN

TEA AND MUSIC BY THE RIVER

Rosewood tea garden attracted more and more visitors each year. Walkers flocked in to sit in the sun by the river and tuck into Mum's generous homemade scones and cakes. It was the ideal stopping point when on their way over Loughrigg or up Langdale via Elterwater. I loved those mornings, the glorious smell of baking and always a 'squiggle' of scone for me to eat, but we all had to help. Our tasks were putting out the 'Morning Coffee and Afternoon Tea' signs at the bottom gate, stacking shelves with sweets and pop (we loved that), and washing up, which we didn't like and usually grumbled about – though as Dad said, if we wanted to go out and play we had to 'toe the line.' He was always full of naval jargon.

If Mum wasn't working or napping she was playing the piano. Customers were highly entertained. They would linger on the terrace, tea gone cold, listening to her. She could play anything from Chopin to New York Stride. I can see her slender fingers now flying across the keys. Two of my favourites were '*My Very Good Friend the Milkman*' and '*The Spider and the Fly*', which I begged her to play over and over until I couldn't keep my eyes open. She played and sang most nights for us before going to bed unless she had visitors staying.

Thorald Bestwick was one of the first paying guests. He visited Skelwith to go fishing on Elterwater and Loughrigg Tarn with his friend, Chuck Bamforth. Mum and he struck up a close long-lasting friendship and he became a regular visitor. Mrs Herman and her daughter Pat from Liverpool became regulars at Rosewood. Pat, like Mum, was also an animal lover and always bought her little dog to stay with her. She became a tremendous supporter of Mum's animal charities. Many others followed and the house was always full. I remember having to move out of the sitting room when guests returned from their days touring the Lakes. Everything had to be 'shipshape and Bristol fashion' according to Dad. Mum worked hard. Up with the blackbirds, baking, sweeping the terrace, changing and washing bedding. There were always linen sheets and shirts soaking in the bath. They had to be rinsed and squeezed out by hand to be hung out on the washing line. It was a busy time. I often saw her sitting with her eyes closed until the bell in the shop rang and she'd heave herself out of the chair to go and serve another customer. At the end of each day she'd go for a walk up to the Force, Park Fell or over Loughrigg – just a stroll to her.

Kerry, Judith and Kim on bottom lawn, Rosewood

Mum always believed, 'A house is not a home without animals.' And the first to arrive at Rosewood was Kim, a black Labrador cross. He came from Harry Wilson's farm under Loughrigg. He was gentle and Mum's constant companion. During the quiet season from October to Easter, they walked the fells together. Lakeland mist has a habit of descending quickly and she was often caught out and didn't get home until after dark. I think she felt safe with Kim. The second animal arrived one stormy day when Kim appeared through the door with something dripping from his mouth. This was Fiddle, a very bedraggled fluffy tabby cat he'd rescued from the flooded river. They settled into family life at Rosewood, enjoying whatever fell from ours and visitors' plates. More animals followed, usually abandoned or found wandering, and from then on there was always a stray cat or a box of kittens in the airing cupboard or under a bed. Locals began ringing Mum if they'd seen stray animals wandering around. They called her the 'animal lady'. Rosewood began to turn into a sanctuary, and not just for animals!

Once again Dad returned home and this time got a job working with Edward Chance, an old friend from naval days. Edward owned Belle Isle on Lake Windermere and together they managed the woods, which enabled Dad to have a log round. Mum would often row across Lake Windermere in all weathers from Bowness Bay to take Dad lunch. Dad took work wherever he could.

In 1956 *Now and Forever* was being filmed in the Lake District. Perhaps Dad was on the 'extras' list, I'm not sure; but I know that Mum, Dad, Patrick, Judith and myself were filmed holding hands and walking across Waterhead Bay. We did this over and over again. At the time I didn't know why but gathered that it was important. When I bought the film many years later that scene had been cut! The following year, *The*

Granny & Kerry playing shop

One that Got Away was also filmed in the Lake District. This was a story about a German prisoner of war who escaped and was chased across Grizedale Forest. Dad was called in to do some stunt driving. He had to race his pickup truck down the Wrynose hillside. I vaguely remember hearing him coming home late and talking about his exciting days spent with the film crew. Eventually, we watched these films at the Ambleside Cinema (now the very smart Zeffirellis). Other films showing then were *Lorna Doone*, *Singin' in the Rain* and of course, Disney's *Cinderella, Peter Pan* and my favourite, *Calamity Jane*. I wanted to be Doris Day and hang up gingham curtains in my den by the river. After going to the cinema, our treat was to stroll up Peggy Hill to the chippy. With our newspaper-wrapped dinner hot in our hands, we'd walk quickly back down to sit on the Ribble bus station wall and eat our chips while we waited for the last bus home.

Judith with Blossom

These were happy occasions, but even though Mum tried really hard to make her new life work, her marriage was still difficult. I remember clearly one night Dad took me to the cinema in Ambleside. After the film, he told me he was just slipping into the Golden Rule to see a friend and that I must sit outside on the bench and not move. Later, a long time later, he appeared looking very unsteady and red faced. I didn't understand his behaviour, this wasn't my Dad, he was scaring me. I don't know how we got home but when we did, Mum was very angry. I felt somehow I was to blame because they argued even more.

One afternoon all three of us were sent out into the garden to play. We couldn't avoid hearing Dad and Mum shouting and banging around. It seemed to go on and on and sounded very serious. When peace finally resumed, we were allowed back in. They behaved as if nothing at all had happened, but were silent and stern and we felt committed to behave. Again I saw Dad making an effort: using his charm to sweeten Mum, cooking meals, helping around the house, calling Mum Kitty. Then one drinking night was the final straw. Mum must have told him to leave because he disappeared for what seemed forever but was only about two years. Mum told me he'd gone to sea. I missed him and cried night after night imagining he'd drowned in storms. Years later I realised he was a war-wounded man trying very hard to change.

Winters were lean times. No tourists, so no money coming in, and no social benefits. It was a hard task to find enough dinner money for the three of us. Mum would scrape around on Monday mornings to find enough pennies and halfpennies for us to take to school. She must have wondered what to do next. I often lied when I arrived at school, saying I'd forgotten it.

These incidents were hidden from those who entered Mum's door. I wonder if they only saw the romantic side of her life?

Chapter Nineteen

A CLIMBER ARRIVES

It was the summer of 1959 and Mum was going about her usual business when a very handsome young man walked up the steps and into the shop. He looked a little like Richard Burton with his short brown hair and gentle blue eyes. In a Lancashire accent he announced, 'I'm Roy Brown and I've ridden up from Saddleworth. My bike's broken down, it's out there on the corner.'

Mum asked him where he was heading and if he had somewhere to live. 'I was going up to Wall End Barn, Langdale, hoping to doss down there.'

Mum looked him up and down. 'Well, you'd better come and stay with us until you get sorted.'

Mum's invitation was the kindness Roy needed. His love for the fells grew to the extent that he never returned to live near Manchester again. He thrived in his new life, running Rock Climbing and Mountaineering courses from Rosewood. I remember his amusing language and how he made up names for things. He affectionately called Mum 'Joggins' and it stuck.

Roy on the fells

However, one afternoon Dad unexpectedly returned home. Roy was kneeling on the shop floor concentrating on making a stronger frame for the counter when he felt something cold pressing into his head. Very slowly he turned and came eye to eye with the barrel of a gun.

'Who the hell are you and what the hell are you doing?' Dad yelled, furious at the intrusion of a young man in the house. Roy kept calm, and with some serious persuasion managed to talk Dad round and remove the gun. After two years at Rosewood, Roy went to live in a bothy on Park Fell.

Friendships, love affairs and plans began and ended at Rosewood. It became a haven for climbers, musicians, artists – people from all walks of life. Perhaps it was the unusual bungalow, or the convenient location for the Langdale valley; but whatever the lure, Rosewood proved an excellent meeting place to exchange adventures over endless large brews of sweet tea. There were always muddy boots, ropes and crampons stacked by the front door. Evenings were filled with tales of those who 'got gripped' on Pavey Arc, the discovery of new climbing routes, the 'v diffs' and the nights lost in mist, reminiscent of Mable Barker's days. The climbing lads, including Barry Kershaw, Jim Cooper and Rob

Jones, renowned for their pub brawls, got up to all sorts of mischief. Mum was ignorant of Patrick's escapades, particularly when he went climbing using her washing line for a rope, and someone once stole a Ribble Bus from Dungeon Ghyll, raced it down the Langdale valley and dumped it at Elterwater! Most of them had motorbikes and used to rev up and down the valley, often crashing on the sharp corner outside our house. It became the norm for the police to knock on our door in the middle of the night. However, despite all the anxiety this might have caused, I think the comings and goings of these crag rats, students and city escapees kept Mum on her youthful toes. Even though I thought her quite old, she was still only in her forties.

* * *

The phone keeps ringing and ringing today – people wanting a cat or puppy or to re-home pets because they are moving house, dying or unable to cope. I'm finding it difficult to actually say the words: 'I'm sorry, Mrs Callaghan doesn't live here any more.' It won't sink in, even though the house is empty and I'm saying it over and over. It deepens my feeling of loss and reminds me of one night years ago.

CHAPTER TWENTY

MISSING

There were definite tourist seasons in those days. The Lake District went quiet from October until Easter when shops reopened and all the vacancy signs went up. During this time, throughout the winter months, Mum togged up in trousers, anorak and sturdy walking boots. Her survival kit amounted to her rucksack (packed with a flask of strong black coffee and a few mints) and her trusty companion Kim. (Fleeces and designer rain-proofs hadn't yet arrived in Ambleside.) She took to the hills and walked for hours, sometimes days. This was her time to enjoy the freedom, fresh air and magnificent views over the land she loved. She'd become an experienced fell walker and always found her way back home. But not this time.

We arrived home from school. No Mum. It was going dark. We waited. Dad lit a fire and made a drink and some toast for us, but I could sense fear, tell something wasn't right. It was far too quiet.

Patrick was first to speak: 'Where's Mum?' Judith started to cry and then I knew something was very wrong. The house felt strange without Mum. I wondered what had happened. Where was she? We couldn't see Loughrigg through the blanket of mist. House lights were just visible across the river. I began to panic. Dad decided to ring the Hawkshead police station. At that moment Roy walked through the door. All previous aggravation between the two men instantly fell away. The seriousness of the situation took over. It was pitch black and had begun raining heavily. There was still no sign of Mum. Roy reckoned she'd gone walking up Langdale, so the police sent out a search party headed by Roy carrying every torch he could find.

'For more than five hours on Wednesday night, police from Lancashire and Westmorland searched the Dungeon Ghyll area of the Langdale Valley after a Skelwith Bridge man had reported his wife missing.'

It transpired that Mum had walked over Langdale, and due to bad weather had decided to stay the night at Mr William Tyson's farm at Watendlath. Unfortunately their telephone was out of order so she was unable to contact home until the following morning. The thought of losing Mum made us all aware of how precious she was. We made a big effort to please her for weeks afterwards.

NIGHT SEARCH ON MOUNTAIN

But "Missing" Wife Was Safe

For more than five hours on Wednesday night police from Lancashire and Westmorland searched the Dungeon Ghyll area of Langdale after a Skelwith Bridge man had reported his wife missing. Unknown to the police, who used searchlights and tracker dogs in the search, she had reached a farm near Watendlath Tarn.

Mrs. Irene Kathleen Rosemary Callaghan, Rosewood, Skelwith Bridge, set off from her home at 10 a.m. on Wednesday to go for a walk with her dog. At 8-30 p.m. she had not returned and Mr. Callaghan informed the police at Hawkshead. It was found that Mrs. Callaghan had caught a bus to Dungeon Ghyll, and had last been seen walking up the hillside. The police started a search which was eventually called off at 2-30 a.m. yesterday (Thursday).

At 8-30 a.m. yesterday Mr. Callaghan received a telephone call that all was well. His wife had stayed the night at Mr. William Tyson's farm at Watendlath.

TELEPHONE OUT OF ACTION

Mr. Callaghan said yesterday (Thursday) that his wife had tried to get into communication with him on the previous night, but the telephone at Watendlath Farm was out of order. "She is a very experienced walker and we did not start to worry until it began to get dark," he said. Mr. Callaghan added that even so it was unusual for his wife to spend all day out walking, and there was heavy rain that night.

CHAPTER TWENTY-ONE

TWO FLY THE NEST

Patrick's Graduation Day, 1965

In October 1959 Patrick left home for Huddersfield Technical College, where he spent six months before moving on for work experience in the laboratories at Storey Brothers in Lancaster. Mum worried after he'd gone but was immensely proud to see him pass his 'A' levels then qualify for the Manchester Institute of Science and Technology to study textile chemistry. After he graduated with a PhD in 1965, he left for Canada to undertake a year's fellowship. More work experience followed and a further four-year fellowship at Birmingham University.

Judith left home to study Art and Graphic Design at Blackpool School of Art, where she met a young man called Peter Tomlinson known as 'Tom'. I was alone in the nest and about to start at the newly-opened John Ruskin School in Coniston. I remember feeling very nervous at the prospect of a large secondary modern school.

Shortly after my first two terms I met an artist called Steve Darbishire. It was July, the summer holidays. I got a job working for Martin Buckmaster who owned the Walnut Coffee Bar in Ambleside. As I was serving at the counter, a man walked in. He looked different from all the other guys, wore jeans and a leather waistcoat. Martin told me he was an artist from Coniston called Steve. I couldn't get him out of my head. A few days later I contrived to miss my bus home in the hope that he would give me a lift. Luckily for me, he did. I told Mum about him and she thought it would be a good idea for him to paint my portrait. This was carried out in his studio at Little Arrow, Coniston. I loved this time. Sitting in the privacy of a real artist's studio listening to Ray Charles and Margie Hendricks! I felt very sophisticated. Mum approved of the finished painting, so commissioned him to paint Judith's portrait. He became a family friend but was forbidden to see me again on a regular basis as Mum said I was far too young to be going out with him. I was thirteen years old and devastated.

Portrait of Kerry painted by Steve in 1961

CHAPTER TWENTY-TWO

THE FLOOD

The late summer of 1962 brought the highest flood anyone in the valley had ever seen. Mum anxiously rushed around calling and bringing her animals inside to safety. Roads were awash and traffic stopped. Steve was working a coal round for Harry Mawson in Ambleside at the time and could only deliver to accessible properties. The water was rising fast. Steve had to get back to Skelwith quickly or be stranded. He managed the flood at Rothay Bridge and drove through Clappersgate, Brathay, past Nanny Brow and Ashley Green. Then, round the corner as he approached Half Way House, the water was so high he had to abandon his truck and walk the last mile or so very carefully and finally negotiate the bridge wall in order to reach the garden gate at Rosewood, water swirling around his knees. The river continued to rise quickly and soon was licking the top step of the house. As far as we could see towards Ambleside, the valley was a lake. Deck chairs, tables and bikes rattled in the cellar; to which Mum said, 'As long as we don't take off like an ark!' and laughed. She thought this was exciting stuff.

A journalist called Mason from the *Chronicle* wrote an article on August 25th, 1962 describing his walk from Ambleside to Grasmere during that time:

'It was the week-end of the Lakeland floods. We could not get through from Ambleside to Skelwith Bridge, a distance of only two and three-quarter miles, until after six o'clock on the Saturday evening. Even then we found the early morning bus stuck near the bridge, under which the River Brathay roared and foamed, while higher up at the Force, it plunged, reared and sprayed itself out angrily over rocks unaccustomed to being submerged. Yet, on the Sunday morning we stood in the sunshine on the lawn of Rosewood, admiring a lump of tree trunk, five feet long by about eighteen inches diameter which had arrived unexpectedly on the flood and settled in the garden. As usual, Mrs Callaghan made it welcome, while we planned its future as a piece of rustic   *furniture'.*

Mum always welcomed new arrivals as an exciting challenge – be it people, animals or objects! She was never flustered regarding severe weather conditions, or at least it never showed.

Flooded garden

Chapter Twenty-Three

DIARY EXTRACTS – 1963

The following winter was harsh. Mum couldn't wait to get out with her new Pentax camera and spent that January walking amongst glaciers on the fells. She kept a five-year diary. These are some extracts:

January 9th, 1963
Fabulous day, up Steel Fell from Dunmail, past Gibson Knott and down Far Easedale, 30ft icicles, glaciers everywhere. V. cold.

January 10th
Went up Walna Scar over top – Dow Crag – high wind.

January 15th
Joan came for day with Andrew. Skated on Barngates, Kerry came after school.

January 21st
Stan Hill, the caretaker of the Skelwith School, was found dead in his chair; his wife was without food all week because of the severe icy conditions. The water pump froze under the house so we had to collect water by breaking ice in the river.

January 31st
George Cook, Vergy and Sylvia from the pottery in Ambleside came for old apple tree – an experiment to make glaze. Judith brought a boy called Tom home. Tarns frozen, roads bad.

February 6th
Thick snow, still no water.

February 13th
Managed to get through to Kendal to the lunch time concert. Lovely.

February 18th
Wonderful day. To Grisedale Tarn, met Outward Bound school up
Dollywagon, continued with Geoff (instructor) up Helvellyn, Raise,
Keppel Cove down to Sticks Pass. Marvellous.

March 23rd
Kerry and I went to see 'Mary Rose', Ambleside Players, St. Anne's
Hall. V good, lift back.

March 28th
Went to Tupperware party at Edie Peppers. Arranged one for myself.

April 11th
Four men came for Easter. Judith off to Wales and Tom went with
Joan in car. Received sad news from Phil Sowerby, his little baby
Jeanie Sue was found dead, acute Bronchial pneumonia.

April 16th
Went to Chris Bonington Eiger lecture. V. good.

April 24th
Lovely day. Busy. Watched Princess Alexandra's wedding on T.V. at
Ruth's.

May 3rd
My birthday. Went to Joan's, met Judith in Kirkham, went to see
Tosca at Opera House with Mum, Joan, Judith, Nigel and Chris
Richardson.
Lovely evening, went back to Mum's, champagne, salmon etc.

May 22nd
Fairly busy. Gardening. Anniversary of Barry's death.

September 11th
Planning permission from Board granted for extension. Heard from
Jim Cliffe.

October 12th
Flowers from Dan.

November 23rd
Terrible news of President Kennedy's assassination yesterday.

It seems very strange to be reading Mum's writing in this small scuffed five-year diary from so long ago. It still carries a sweet smell. Her remembering Barry. Dad still in love with her, even though by then they were divorced, he was still sending flowers, saying 'sorry'. These memories and images are so clear to me, as if they're recent entries. I can see all these people, hear their voices. I can remember how Mum dressed and behaved, always energetic, slim and stunning in her cotton floral sun dresses and skirts which she wore most days around the house. They seemed to have yards of material in which to bury my head. I see her, in between customers, rushing onto the top lawn to drop her shoulder straps and lie in the sun. Sometimes she wore linen blouses and trousers – mostly for walking.

Aware that other villagers were beginning to open tea gardens and B&B's, Mum thought it was time to up her game.

* * *

To accommodate the increasing number of walkers who normally sat in the sitting room, Mum decided she would like to build a café on the river side of the house. In this same year, 1963, a planning application was sent in. The good news of approval came on September 11th. Tom, Judith's boyfriend, offered to do the building work, but anyone who turned up was co-opted into digging or mixing cement. Mum also spent any spare time clearing and shovelling earth in preparation for laying foundations. She wasn't afraid of getting her hands dirty. The café took just over a year to build and was a great asset to her business. Walkers could take tea inside, with a beautiful view of the river through the large windows. They sat on built-in red seats lined around the walls. The tables were Fabloned with the prettiest designs Mum could find. It was a difficult job to avoid creasing when laying new Fablon on the tables, but Mum didn't worry too much about that, it was so much easier to keep clean than constantly washing tablecloths. Dad had nothing to do with this project. He was forbidden to come home, although for some reason I was allowed to spend a day with him on Windermere Lake. I loved that day. Judith told me he was working at the telephone exchange in Kendal at the time because according to Mum's diary she'd met him several times in Kendal for lunch.

The house continued to buzz with friends. Jim and Kay Phelan called whenever they were passing through but never stayed more than three nights. It was a code amongst the vagabonds never to outstay their welcome. This kept regular doors open.

A day with Dad on Windermere Aug 1963

A couple from Liverpool called Jim and Oona Cliffe began visiting Rosewood and became good friends. He was an artist and member of the Bluecoat Chambers, painting mostly portraits. During the Autumn he painted Mum's portrait. They were one couple of many who returned year after year to spend afternoons sitting in the garden at Rosewood.

It was rare for Mum to go out but sometimes she'd spend her days with Phyllis Ashton in Staveley, or they'd meet for coffee in Ambleside. And occasionally when Granny drove up from Worsley, she would take Mum out for lunch or tea at the Swan Hotel in Newby Bridge or the

Jim & Oona Cliffe in the garden at Rosewood

Langdale Chase at Windermere. Sometimes she took us all out for dinner at the Skelwith Bridge Hotel. We had to dress smartly and be on our best behaviour. I remember feeling terribly embarrassed when once she sent the plates back to the kitchen because they were cold. But I loved those days when relations visited. It meant a ride in a car or a delicious tea somewhere, and Mum became less strict, more relaxed. On rainy Wednesdays if she thought there would be little trade, she would catch a bus to Kendal for the lunchtime concerts held in the town hall. A diary entry on November 20th read: 'Lovely day. Went to hear Chinese pianist in Kendal. Went to Abbott Hall to see Eskimo exhibition of Art. Sale viewing'. It turned out she went back to that sale and bought a new gas cooker for £36! (Gas cylinders were supplied by Mr Retallick of Ambleside.) Mum cooked the most remarkable meals for endless numbers of people on that stove. Often I noticed she would go without if there wasn't enough to go round, although she was brilliant at making a little go a long way. Even if she had few ingredients she used to make us fritters – a mixture of flour and water or milk and egg if she had any, with various flavours. Savoury would be made with thyme or curry powder. Sweet ones were made by adding sugar, currants and spices.

It was very important to Mum that the family should be together at Christmas. This naturally included friends. The house never ceased to be full. Preparations began in November with the baking of large fruit cakes and making mincemeat. A huge box of apples would arrive from Auntie Joan and Uncle Jos in Freckleton. Presents of money came from Great Aunt Noel (Dad's Aunt) who lived in London. I never met her but always had to write her thank-you letters. We made all our decorations: paper chains, bells and nativity scenes. On Christmas Eve we would wrap up, and in the chill misty air rising from the river, walk over to the Skelwith Bridge Hotel for drinks and celebration. We sang carols accompanied by someone on piano and everyone was very merry.

There was always a large brightly-lit tree outside the main door. I used to gaze at it from our shop window. It was magical. Afterwards we would spin out our supper as long as we could – too excited to go to bed. I don't know how Mum managed to fill our pillow cases with presents, put up decorations and prepare everything for dinner. I remember my presents consisted of Pop-it beads to make necklaces and bracelets, plastic make up sets with mirror, a tangerine, chocolates and books: favourites included the Lavender Blue nursery rhyme book, *Heidi*, and *Lassie*. Every year Mum bought a large turkey from Claytons butchers in Ambleside. There never failed to be at least fifteen family and friends around the evening table decorated with sugared almonds, dates and nuts, tucking into all the trimmings, then after a large flaming pudding, Mum would produce a small box of Sobranie cocktail cigarettes to hand round. It was the only time I saw her smoke. On Christmas Eve 1963 there was a heavy snowfall in the night. It was a wonderful sight in the morning. We all rushed out to sledge and throw snowballs. I remember the silence of no traffic.

As the years went on and Mum grew more tired, Judith came back home to help her with the Christmas celebrations.

1964 had its ups and downs beginning with a motorbike accident. On 12th January Patrick hit a sheep at Clappersgate near Ambleside and came off his bike. He had a lucky escape but had to go to Manchester hospital for stitches on his eye. Shortly after, on 24th January, Bob Williams died. No more fishing. The village wasn't the same without him. Many more of our older neighbours began to pass away; the village was changing.

Mum kept busy and Rosewood continued to be fully booked with visitors. She decided to buy an old four-berth 'Eccles' caravan. Foundations were dug and laid in the back garden to house the caravan. It fitted in perfectly next to a very old apple tree. The rent was between eight and ten guineas a week. Visitors loved staying in the caravan, with just the sound of birdsong and the river. Peggy and Aidan Rowlands and their children were amongst the first to book in. Mum and Peggy became good friends and sometimes, if trade was good, Peggy helped Mum in the café. They returned year after year. Her daughter, Stephanie, told me they loved being able to walk out of the back gate through the woods and up to Skelwith Force.

The Eccles caravan

With the new café extension, Mum was thrilled to be able to accommodate more afternoon teas, but it increased her work load so that she couldn't manage alone. She employed young girls to help out. Many returned for years after, bringing their children to see Mum.

Her creativity and energy never dampened. One spring she set to building a miniature waterfall and stream behind the house running into a pond edging the river to replicate a Japanese garden. It involved more digging and moving an apple tree and some rocks around. Water was pumped up from the river and made a lovely sound until the pump broke down, which it often

Building the miniature waterfall in the back garden

did much to Mum's annoyance. I thought it odd to want this when she already had the sight and sound of the Brathay running by, but she loved to watch fish swimming amongst her water lilies and irises. She planted a weeping willow next to the pond but this died, I think because the roots ran into the side of the well. I bought her a beautiful maple to replace it, which still thrives. Tom continued to help out in the garden with mowing and keeping the paths clear. By this time, he and Judith were dating seriously, until one day he suddenly disappeared to Jersey with Steve, leaving Judith heartbroken and Mum livid. Perhaps it was his thinking time – because when he eventually returned, he and Judith married on March 6th, 1965 at the Registrar's office in Kendal. Later that year I left school.

Judith & Tom

I'd been dating a lad for nearly a year when, after taking me to a Beatles concert in Blackpool, he suddenly announced we were finished. I thought my world had ended. Mum kindly suggested I go and stay for a while with Dad, who was living in Blackheath, London. It was 1964, early November when she asked Steve to escort me on the bus to Victoria Station.

The Manbys, having left Mill Brow in 1963, were also living in Blackheath and invited Steve and me to a bonfire. That night Steve and I fell in love. Reluctantly I had to travel back north, as Mum had informed me, 'You need something to fall back on so I've enrolled you at the Allen Technical College in Kendal for a year's secretarial course.' I was furious. All I wanted was to float around in my bell-bottom jeans being an artist or a singer with Steve. But he was determined to stay in London and make his fortune in the folk business. I spent my last year at Rosewood and tension between Mum and me made it a difficult one.

I behaved badly, biding time. I couldn't wait to leave college. As soon as my course was over, I left for the lights of London. I remember how sad Mum looked waving me off at Ambleside bus station, the last child gone. Perhaps she was secretly jumping for joy! Whether she felt happy or sad, times were definitely on the move again.

During the following years grandchildren arrived: Dylan on August 18th 1965, and Sean on December 17th 1966 to Judith and Tom. They then moved back north to live in Ambleside where, on November 16th 1968, their daughter Emma Jane was born.

It was Christmas and the turn of 1967 when all the family gathered at Rosewood. It pleased Mum to have everyone back under her roof. After all the celebrations, Judith and Tom then returned to High Wycombe with their two sons, Dylan and Sean, and on 4th January, Steve and I reluctantly travelled back to London. We'd wanted to stay to watch Donald Campbell break the World Speed Record on Coniston Water especially as Steve and his family were friends of Donald. Steve had taken me to meet him the night before and during the conversation he turned to me and said, 'You know I'm going to die tomorrow don't you.' I was shocked and speechless. When we arrived back at our Putney flat, we received the awful news of his death. We both felt too far from home. There was more sad news to follow.

Feeling homesick, I rang Mum on January 9th to see how she was. It was heart breaking to hear her miles away sobbing on the end of the phone, telling me that her faithful companion Kim had died.

'He just walked out onto into the snow-filled path and lay down,' she told me. Kim was the grand old age of twenty.

On March 15th, Steve and I married in Brathay Church. The newly repaired church bells rang out, especially for our day. There was an icy wind coming off the tops as Cedric Dand drove us in his landau filled with daffodils. He took us from the church back to the Skelwith Bridge Hotel for a reception. Granny and aunts and uncles from both sides of the family travelled up for the wedding and all had a terrific time. Mum looked glamorous in her coffee-coloured silk dress and matching pill-box hat. Dad didn't turn up and I remember feeling terribly disappointed, but I realise now that being in the close company of Mum's relations would have proved too awkward for him. Champagne flowed and during the evening party Roy met Steve's sister Elizabeth. They fell in love and married in October, 1969.

Steve & Kerry's wedding 15th March '67

Kay at Ibby & Roy's wedding - 25th Oct '69

Steve and I had two daughters: Rebecca, born in 1968, and Naomi in 1971. Patrick and Jenni married on 29th December 1977 in Barrow. Two more grandchildren arrived – Anna in 1981 and Simon in 1982. There was plenty of baby-sitting for Mum. She loved the house full of children. They often stayed for the weekend and had a wonderful time while we were renovating our houses. Mum would take Rebecca, Naomi and Emma for walks through the woods looking for fairies' homes in the trees. Rebecca and Naomi remember Granny bringing them breakfast in bed: 'We had All-Bran smothered in warm milk and toast with lumps

Patrick & Jenny's wedding
29th December 1977

of 'joggolade' (Mum's marmalade) which we had to spread with our fingers. As soon as Granny left the room, we tipped our bowls out of the window, where the dogs scoffed it up. One day she caught us. She didn't say anything, just never gave it to us again.

Mum understood children, she made them feel safe and they loved being around her. She also instilled a love of animals in all the grandchildren. There were always three or four dogs, and also eight to a dozen cats lying in front of the fire and on the mantelpiece. They either just arrived on the doorstep or were purposely abandoned. Mum never turned them away. Feeding time was hilarious. Trying to place all those saucers on the floor at the same time! But because of the café and all the food preparation, the health inspectors were very concerned and kept arriving to tell Mum to cover up her cakes and stop cats jumping around the kitchen. Mum took no notice of these 'silly little rules' as she called them. Eventually she put a notice on all the tables saying that all proceeds went to the animals, and if people didn't like them, would they like to go somewhere else! Most stayed and thoroughly enjoyed the company of dogs and cats!

* * *

Patrick, Judith and I decide it's time to put some life back into the old house, make it more welcoming for the family to stay. During the next few weeks we replace most of the old carpets and lay new lino in the hallway, kitchen and bathroom. We take away the old redundant shop counter and return the little room to its original use. The piano is a bit beyond any help so we leave it alone. We paint walls, clean windows and buy ready-made curtains and wash all the bedding. The dresser, tables and chairs soak up several jars and tins of polish. It feels such a positive thing to do, and a nice surprise when we bring Mum home for the day, although she might not notice the changes. Mum is very pleased to hear that members of the family are staying in her house.

Chapter Twenty-Four

HONEYPOT

The old upright piano was beginning to fall to pieces, so with great excitement, on September 17th 1964 Mum went to the Kendal auction rooms and purchased a burr walnut Ronisch baby grand piano. There was quite a kerfuffle a week later when the new picture window in the sitting room had to be taken out for the piano to be hauled in. It was a beautiful musical instrument and was played regularly by two very accomplished pianists from Lancaster, Derek Drake and Gordon Fox. They spent hours playing classical, blues, jazz and boogie-woogie. These sessions sometimes lasted for days and the house rocked! Sadly not every day was a party. I remember how shocked Mum was when she heard that Derek had tragically drowned in Lake Windermere.

While Gordon was training at George Cook's pottery at the Old Mill in Ambleside, he lived at Rosewood. He and Mum spent many days walking the fells. When Gordon met and married Barbara Turner, he moved out to rent Low Arnside farmhouse. After a few very cold winters, they found a house at Skelwith Fold where he set up his first pottery. They had two sons, Matthew and Rupert, and returned frequently to Rosewood. Gordon continued to come down to Rosewood to practise the piano while the children played in the garden and river.

Gordon, Barbara & Matthew Fox making pots at Skelwith Fold 1967

Phil Sowerby was an extremely flamboyant character who arrived from near Manchester. He and his wife Eileen, whom everyone called Elf, took Mum out to hotels for fairly extravagant meals – often on the spur of the moment. He was a potter, great fun and played trombone at the impromptu jam sessions at Rosewood's weekend parties. (Unfortunately he disappeared under the shadow of owing some locals money, obviously due to his lavish lifestyle. He was never seen in the area again.) Some of these parties ended in arguments and fights, like the one on New Year's Eve. I remember a very heated argument concerning politics and unions. Someone had mouthed off too much and ended up on the kitchen floor very battered and bruised. He had to be escorted out and the party came to an abrupt end.

Rosewood continued to be a hub – there was always someone new drinking a brew in the sitting room when I came home from school.

We discovered that Rosewood had a 'sister' wooden house in Newlands, Keswick. This was Rigg Beck and became known as 'the purple house' where Vergi Vergauen, another potter at George Cook's, lived with his wife Varya and their children. Musicians, artists, writers and actors including Bob Hoskins drifted between there and Rosewood during this time. Mum loved all this activity and was always off somewhere with someone. I could tell she had many admirers and love affairs. But there were also tears. Even though her heart must have been broken many times, she found solace in walking the tops, with family, her beloved animals and home. Mum cared deeply for her surroundings especially when they took a battering from extreme weather conditions. Apart from floods, wind was also a worry with the house being surrounded by old tall trees. I found this amongst Mum's papers:

Death of an old friend

For nigh on a century, had grown from a tiny seedling to thirty metres high. With enormous strength he had done battle with the elements, and defied them. Who was to know when his great heart started to die.

One night a fearful storm came, he could no longer fight, his huge trunk split as the wind shrieked thru' his branches, slowly, with a long sigh he bent and fell, held between two slender silver birches he lay silently by the river, whose waters he had watched for many decades. Quiet memories of the songs of birds in his branches, children playing around his great trunk, beloved animals buried at his feet. The sadness of his death and all his memories, carried by fast flowing waters, along the river banks and down to the lake.

But we are left unhurt and remembering.'

This was written by Mum after the fall of a pine tree in the back garden. It fell parallel to the river, luckily just missing the house.

The following years flowed on much the same: visitors stayed, friends dropped in with their husbands, wives and children. The top lawn was often filled with children playing on the swing.

The café thrived and at Easter and Whitsuntide I would drive over to help out. The pots would pile up and all had to be washed up by hand, there was no room to install a dishwasher. I knew Mum's energy levels were not as high as before and she needed more rest. She began closing the café and shop on unpromising days. On one particularly wet day in 1972 a young boy walked into the café. This first meeting with Mum and Rosewood changed his life.

Jan Cooper & Kay in the kitchen

CHAPTER TWENTY-FIVE

NICHOLAS

In a letter to me Nicholas wrote:

It was pouring down. My parents, who holidayed in a caravan up at Skelwith Fold, had gone walking to Elterwater. I didn't want to go with them and was standing in the pouring rain on the other side of the river when I spotted the 'Rosewood Tea Gardens' sign. I trotted over the bridge and into the café. While Kay was making tea, I peered through the door. It seemed intensely interesting. First I saw the old grandfather clock, then a bust of someone on the window and then, with great excitement I saw the piano. Anything to do with pianos had a magnetic effect. I forgot my lunch and when Kay returned she noticed me looking and asked if I played. I said I was learning and was very keen.

"Would you like to turn the pages of this piece while I play it for you?" We sat down together at her old Ronisch baby grand and she played Liszt's Un Sospiro. This was a revelation. That single musical event was one of the most moving, thrilling and exciting musical experiences I have ever had. It placed my childish love of music onto an entirely different plane, combined, as it was, with the novelty of a new and unexpected turn of events from the prospect of a rather boring, melancholy picnic in the rain into something deeply and permanently transforming.

From that day on Nicholas regularly visited Rosewood to practise the piano in return for washing up. 'It is a tribute to your mother that she was able to treat me as an equal person.'

I have lovely memories of walking up the garden path to the sound of Nicholas practising the piano. He was always smiling, enthusiastic and so polite. It was he who told me he once asked Mum why Dr Who was in her garden. I later learned that her former boyfriend Jon Pertwee must have paid a visit.

Nicholas Ashton & Kay, Queen's Hall Edinburgh, May 1ˢᵗ '97

During this time Mum was making frequent journeys to Worsley to be with Granny, who'd been diagnosed with cancer. On 1st June 1972 Steve and I drove Mum to Woodstock Drive. I remember walking into a dim hall that smelt of apples and tea. Auntie Joan and others were in the sitting room; they were quiet and looked solemn. Someone said I should go upstairs to sit with Granny. I stood at her bedroom door and peered into the gloom. All I could see was a cloud of white hair on the pillow and her small outline under the counterpane. I listened to her slow breath echoing and was too scared to go any further. When we arrived back at Rosewood that night we got a phone call to say that Granny had died. One Manchester newspaper obituary began, 'By the death on Thursday of Mrs Edith Elise Smith, at her home in Woodstock Drive, Worsley, this area has lost one of its best known personalities and a well-loved voluntary worker to whom many charitable causes owe a debt of gratitude.'

Mum became subdued. Even though the house was still full of friends, she hid her grief, but I often caught her looking bereft. Again, she found love and comfort in her animals and commissioned Steve to paint portraits of them all – Kim, Jess, Beauty, Sheeba, Chippy, until there was no space left on her bedroom wall.

* * *

Frost is lying like ripped paper in pockets of the garden. The leaves have almost gone and the river is flowing high. I stand looking at the piles of Mum's personal effects still to organise. It feels odd and far too quiet now the last of her animals are gone. I can only hear mice scratching in the ceiling and hungry birds at the feeders which I replenish often. The sorting out is endless, I can't believe how much memorabilia Mum has kept. Mine and Judith's old drawings, school exercise books, legal documents and letters stuffed in the chest. An old theatre programme slips from a diary.

• PART THREE •

Chapter Twenty-Six

FOOTLIGHTS OF AMBLESIDE

With the last of her children married and gone from the nest, and with the help of an inheritance from her mother, there was no real need to for Mum to work so hard in the tea garden, and she opened only when she wanted to. I remember some very disappointed customers on her 'closed' days. Even though she'd already turned most of her energy into saving and looking after local dejected animals, she still found time for her old profession and joined the Ambleside Amateur Dramatic Society. This Society was originally formed in 1907, then in 1932 became known as The Ambleside Players. They performed at least one production every year except in 1939. All Wartime productions were in aid of The Red Cross.

In April 1975 Mum took the part of Mrs Bradman in *Blithe Spirit*, produced by Freda Wagstaff. A report in the *Westmorland Gazette* read: 'adding fluidity to the performance were Mike Wagstaff and Kay Callaghan as Dr. and Mrs Bradman – both giving assured performances. The following April, Joyce Cockcroft produced *The Old Man of the Mountains*, a play written by Norman Nicholson. Mum prompted and I played The Beck alongside Barbara Priss and Eileen Smith. It was an honour to meet Mr. Nicholson, who arrived on set one day to see how we were progressing. He was the image of an old man of the mountains, dressed in tweeds with wiry white hair and bushy eyebrows. He looked on and seemed pleased, commenting gently about his play.

Perfect for Players

WHEN an innocent man is the prime suspect in the hunt for his wife's murderer he sets out to find the real culprit.

His search is particularly vital because his arrest is imminent and he has very little time to find the evidence which will clear him.

The situation provided the perfect Who Dunnit? plot and was used to great effect by Ambleside Players in their production of Deadly Record by Nina Warner Hooke in St. Anne's Hall.

The play was bursting with character parts which allowed the cast plenty of scope to use their individual powers of interpretation.

Kay Callaghan was particularly pleasing as the fussy Cockney housekeeper and her amusing lines did much to relieve the tension of the plot.

Aileen Airey was deliciously arty and curious as nosey neighbour Mr Pape, who spent most of her time spying on the people around her. Lynda Wilson as nurse Ann Garfield, was sufficiently protective towards her doctor employer, and had in the end a motive for murder.

Writer, Trevor Hamilton, played by Geoff Halden, refused to accept the blame for a murder he did not commit even in the face of incriminating evidence. With the help of Roberta Hudson, played by Phillipa Ware, he fought convincingly to clear himself.

Andrew Spokes was suitably vigilant as PC Hobbs, while Mike Wagstaff as Det. Supt. Ambrose and Alexander Ross as Det. Sgt. Craig were typically suspicious and thorough in their crime investigations.

The audience was not as plentiful as it should have been for the high standard of performance. The warm welcome from the drama group attended to those who did brave the cold, damp weather, more than made up for the chilly conditions outside. KH

Westmorland Gazette review for 'Deadly Record'

THE OLD MAN OF THE MOUNTAINS

CAST

AHAB	MIKE WAGSTAFFE
OBADIAH	TONY YEADON
REBECCA	LYNETTE HARRIS
MARTHA	ANGELA SIMPSON
RUTH	LYNDA WILSON
BEN	ALAN SMITH
ELIJAH	WILF HUNTER
DAVID	MARTIN TOMLINSON
THE RAVEN	FRANK STRAW
THE BECK	KERRY DERBYSHIRE, BARBARA PRISS, EILEEN SMITH

Prompts .... Kay Callaghan
Prop .... Ann Daysh, Mollie Harrison
Wardrobe ... Barbara Priss, Audrey Ireland
Lighting and Effects .... George Sanders, Alan Stevenson
Stage Crew ... Theo Stevenson, George Sanders

SYNOPSIS OF SCENES

The action of the play takes place in a Cumbrian cottage and garden.

ACT I
A summer morning

ACT II
Half an hour later

Interlude on Carmel Fell

ACT III
Next morning

The old man of the mountains 1976

Old man of the mountains ~ St Anne's Hall, Ambleside 1976

Ambleside Players present ..

Blithe Spirit by Noel Coward produced by Freda Wagstaff in St Anne's Hall

Thursday, Friday & Saturday 10th, 11th & 12th April at 8pm each evening

Date SATURDAY 12 APR 1975

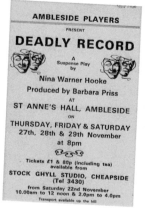

A sparkling success

Westmorland Gazette review by Jane Renouf of 'I have five daughters' ~ Kay centre front

AMBLESIDE PLAYERS
PRESENT

DEADLY RECORD

A Suspense Play by

Nina Warner Hooke

Produced by Barbara Priss

AT

ST ANNE'S HALL, AMBLESIDE

ON

**THURSDAY, FRIDAY & SATURDAY
27th, 28th & 29th November
at 8pm**

Tickets £1 & 80p (including tea) available from

STOCK GHYLL STUDIO, CHEAPSIDE
(Tel 3430)

from Saturday 22nd November
10.00am to 12 noon & 2.0pm to 4.00pm
Transport available up the hill

Colin Wagstaffe & Kay in 'Small Hotel'

In 1978 Mum performed in *A Small Hotel*, then in a 1979 pre-Christmas performance of *I Have Five Daughters*, based on *Pride and Prejudice*. Jane Renouf, reporting for the *Westmorland Gazette*, called it 'A sparkling success. Mrs Bennett connived, sulked, pouted, swaggered and nagged interrupted only occasionally by attacks of the vapours: so complete and masterful was Kay Callaghan's performance'. In November1980, Mum performed in *Deadly Record*, produced by Barbara Priss. In a review: 'Kay Callaghan was particularly pleasing as the fussy Cockney housekeeper and her amusing lines did much to relieve the tension of the plot.'

I remember sitting with Mum by her roaring fire listening to her reciting her lines. Mum would take her rôle and I took all the others. One day she mentioned that she was having difficulty remembering them and didn't think she could continue with the Ambleside Players. But being a 'trouper', Mum continued until April 1981, when she finally played the part of Miss Prism in *The Importance of Being Ernest*, produced by Joyce Cockcroft. Jane Renouf, who played Cecily Cardew, told me that she found Mum's stage-craft tips helpful and said, 'You could tell Kay was a pro' by the instinctive way she knew exactly when to start to speak, for greatest impact.'

Tickets for these plays were available from Fred Holdsworth's Bookshop, Ambleside, and cost £1 or 80p, including tea – less for children and concessions. They were staged in St. Anne's Hall and always to a packed house. There was magic in those evenings when we huddled together in the hall, then walked out chatting and full of excitement into frosty nights with stars glistening over the rooftops of Ambleside.

CHAPTER TWENTY-SEVEN

ANIMAL RESCUE

Granny's death left a huge gap in Mum's life, but not being one to dwell too long in the shadows, she threw herself into a life-long passion. Acutely aware of how tragic and cruel some animals' lives were, she set about doing something to help them – 'all the defenceless creatures who cannot voice their suffering and pain,' she told me.

A letter in the *Westmorland Gazette*, written by the RSPCA, said that they had rescued eight dogs and four cats locally. This was good, but not good enough according to various readers, including Mum. She wrote to the Gazette voicing her view that more should be done to help suffering animals. A week later a lady called Jo Moon responded positively to her letter. Then Judy Potter contacted her. The three women decided to get together and after discussions, in order to improve the situation of unwanted and abandoned animals, they started their own charity. On October 27th 1972, an article, 'New Drive to Rescue Animals' in the *Westmorland Gazette*, talked about the newly-founded organisation. By November, Animal Rescue Registered Charity was formed. In one of Mum's notebooks I found she'd written this: *'To ignore cruelty is to condone it, ANIMAL RESCUE is the Society to which really caring*

people come. The animal being has just as much right to consideration as the human being.'

This small group had no money, no premises, no kennels but a huge mission and kind hearts. I wonder if they realised how huge this would turn out to be? I remember how determined and focused Mum became during that time. The three founders began to save animals by collecting strays and taking them to the safety of their homes, or boarding them out privately. In those days, if strays were taken to police stations, they were kept for one week and if no one claimed them they were destroyed. That was unthinkable for this new organisation – their policy was *'Never to turn away or put down any animal, provided they weren't suffering, and to find good homes for them.'* Newspapers began to take an interest. It was quite a new thing to embark on such a venture; other registered charities were usually large organisations. Publicity started to take a serious role in Animal Rescue and word was spreading. The Carlisle newspaper asked Jo for an interview at her house in Cartmel. With Mum present, they wrote an article and both were photographed with the rescued animals. At the same time they were invited to the House of Commons with other animal charities including the RSPCA. Jo's intended policy suggested that 'animals should have a licence costing £10 for life: this would go towards neutering and stop them breeding.' This seemed a reasonable and sensible option and Mum did her utmost to support it, but no one took it up.

One day, after a journey to Portsmouth to re-home an Old English sheepdog, Jo returned home to a phone call summoning her to Manchester for a television interview. Not missing an opportunity, Jo and Mum went, and in front of the cameras Jo announced that it was essential that anyone who'd lost an animal must contact all police stations because lost dogs can travel a long way and could be anywhere, not just in their locality. Publicity hotted up, their name and reputation began to spread. Phone calls constantly came in regarding strays, and people wanting to give dogs and cats a home, but they were short of kennels to house the unfortunates. Subscriptions were £1 per year and donations trickled in. They found a field near Flookborough and eventually, after much negotiation, the farmer agreed to let them have it. The South Lakeland District Council gave them £500 to erect four kennels and fence the land.

Animal Rescue never made charges but relied on donations and subscriptions, which were pouring in from all over the country. They appealed for feed bowls, bedding, collars, food etc. Mum was their treasurer, and in their first year income totalled £3810.57p collected from jumble sales, coffee mornings, Christmas Fairs and collecting boxes. Mum thought nothing of walking the streets of Ambleside on freezing days and nights collecting from shops and house to house for raffles prizes and tombolas. For their Christmas Fair on December 8th 1973, Mum collected various gifts including anoraks, jumpers, hand cream, pottery etc., all kindly donated by several Ambleside businesses including: Lakeland Knitwear, A.G. Gates, Frank Davies, Bell's Chemist, Old Mill Pottery, Hannah Robinson, Tyson's Shoe Shop, The Rothay Manor Hotel, The Royal Oak, The Waterhead Hotel and many more. Since her mother's passing, she could afford a car and spent all hours driving to wherever there was an animal in distress. Her telephone never stopped ringing, with requests to collect dogs, cats, poultry, donkeys, hedgehogs etc., many of whom were taken into the sanctuary of Rosewood, at least until a suitable home was found. It was this devotion and sheer hard work that kept Animal Rescue going. In a talk Mum gave to a local school in 1976, she told of having saved over a thousand dogs and cats.

Unfortunately problems were brewing over differences of principle. Some decided that the animals in kennels waiting to be homed should be destroyed after a certain time, and others, including Mum, were totally opposed to this believing that every unwanted animal would eventually be placed and funds would be found to support this. Rifts within the committee began to form. From the annual report and statement of accounts for the year ending 31st December 1980, the committee members were: Mr Alfred Wainwright, M.B.E., Chairman; Mum, Vice Chairman; Judy Potter, Hon. Secretary; and Mrs Betty Wainwright, Hon. Treasurer. The final rift – 'money v. policy' – came in 1981. Mr and Mrs Wainwright remained running Animal Rescue, while Mum and others branched off to found a new charity.

Steve and I knew Alfred and Betty Wainwright well (Betty always called him Red). Occasionally they used to babysit Rebecca and Naomi. We'd take them to their house in Kendal and although some might not believe it, as he appeared a solitary man, Alfred would spend hours reading to them, watching television with them and teaching them to play drafts. Sadly, because of the Animal Rescue disagreements and the final split, we saw very little of them after that time.

Chapter Twenty-Eight

ANIMAL CONCERN

As one chapter ended another opened for Mum. Her problem now lay with the Animal Rescue divide. Rosewood was bursting with dogs and cats, either friendly or skirting around each other growling and hissing. She knew there were hundreds of animals still needing homes and didn't hang around waiting.

In 1982 she met with fifteen like-minded people to elect a temporary committee and decide on a name. They registered their new charity: Animal Concern Cumbria, Registered Charity 513091. My husband Steve drew their logo and advertisements were placed in the *Westmorland Gazette* and Echo, but again, there were three ingredients they did not have: kennels for dogs, a cattery, and money for boarding fees, vet fees and advertising. However, three ingredients they certainly had in full supply were enthusiasm, love of animals, and determination to make it work. I remember how Mum was difficult to get hold of as she was always dashing around on animal business. This came before anything else. They managed to open their first cattery at Marton, near Lindal-in-Furness. It cost £1,400 and immediately filled with stray and pregnant cats and kittens that had been dumped in hedges and roadsides. Numerous phone calls flooded in, offering good homes and

Greetings

Animal Concern logo by Stephen Darbishire

donations. Helpers rallied to raise funds with fashion shows, coffee mornings, whist drives, sponsored dog walks and summer fêtes. Fund-raising days became annual events. Strawberry Teas were held by kind permission of their President, Brigadier Tryon and Mrs Wilson at Dallam Tower, who were generous in giving over their beautiful garden and facilities for the day. These were always

Brigadier & Mrs Tryon Wilson with Kay at Dallam Tower ~ Animal Concern Strawberry Tea

well attended. Another annual event was the Rum Butter Tea held at Rosewood. I remember the hustle and bustle of setting up trestle tables in the garden filled with cakes, gifts, clothes etc., praying it wouldn't rain. Mum baked for days beforehand: every tin and cupboard was layered with the wonderful smell of Mum's date and walnut bread, cakes and dozens of scones, cream and homemade jam. (It was my job to make the rum butter.) Trays loaded with cups and saucers were carried outside to the terrace where folk clustered and over-excited dogs ran around waiting for the Dog Show to start in the field opposite the Skelwith Bridge Hotel.

In Decembers, a Christmas Fair would be very kindly held by Brian and Christine Hewitt at the Regent Hotel, Waterhead, Ambleside. Again tables were set with gifts, preserves, sparkling decorations and home baking. We all pitched in helping and donating Christmas cakes etc., and they supplied delicious mince pies and coffee. These events proved very popular and raised generous funds to help many animals. John Tovey from Miller Howe was a keen animal lover and took great interest – generously supporting Animal Concern. He constantly talked

ROSEWOOD TEA GARDEN IS RUN FOR THE SOLE PURPOSE OF RAISING MONEY TO FEED THE UNWANTED DOGS AND CATS RESCUED BY ME. THE HOUSE AND GARDEN ARE THEIR HOME. ANYONE OBJECTING TO MY ANIMALS, I WOULD SUGGEST THEY MIGHT BE HAPPIER HAVING TEA ELSEWHERE. ALL OTHERS ARE WELCOME.

Kay at Rosewood surrounded by her animals

with Mum to keep up to date with how they were doing even after his move to South Africa. Mum never held back on fund-raising. She contacted business people and celebrities she thought able to help; wrote letters to James Herriot, Spike Milligan, Jilly Cooper, David Bellamy and The Sainsbury Trust, to name a few. Most responded favourably. This all helped in helping the unwanted animals.

Rebecca and Naomi remember many occasions when they stayed with Granny at Rosewood for the weekend. The phone would ring or there'd be someone banging on the door in the middle of the night because an animal had been found in distress, run over, or some dreadful cruelty had been discovered. Mum never hesitated to get up and immediately sort these matters out. Sometimes she had very angry callers who threatened her physically because they thought she was interfering. She stood up to them because all that mattered to her was the welfare of the animals.

In 1983, the records show that the number of safely placed animals was: seventy-three dogs, forty-two cats, eleven baby hamsters and one pigeon. However, there were still many waiting patiently in kennels and temporary homes. Rosewood continued to house at least sixteen cats and rarely less than four dogs at any one time. Many needed nursing back to good health. Mum named some of the cats after precious stones: Topaz, Moonstone, and Sapphire who accompanied her on short walks. Sapphire was a lovely character and lived for twenty-one years.

By 1985 Mum was giving weekly broadcasts on Radio Cumbria, reading out names of all the needy animals and appealing for any kind of help. Members of the committee at that time were: Monica Snashell, Jean Wilson, Mo Kenyon, Betty Coyne, Bob Richie, Mrs Millington, Mrs Baber and Doris Hayton, who often accompanied Mum on rescue journeys. The volunteers worked relentlessly, giving their time to give these poor neglected animals a chance. Phone calls with requests to pick up, deliver and rescue were constant. One appeal came from Paul and Jane Renouf. Jane told me, 'I telephoned Kay to say, 'We have a young cat called Tinker who is being bullied by a tom cat who keeps coming in at night, beating

Kay with Beauty

Tinker up and eating his food.' Kay said she'd catch him and have him neutered: then he'd stop behaving like that. The tom was caught and the deed was done.

'What's to stop this stray coming back in?' Paul asked Kay, to which she replied, 'Not likely, would you go back to the place where you'd been caught, taken away, then had your balls chopped off?'

Neutering was the solution to prevent even more unwanted animals, and they encouraged new pet owners to do this. Sometimes the plights of these animals were not just the production of unwanted litters but were unbelievably horrific: dogs purposely locked in sheds to starve to death, or abandoned on motorways; litters of kittens found tied up in bags. There were endless cruelties, yet she dealt with each atrocity with great strength and determination – she never walked away. Mum's diaries weren't filled with birthday or anniversary reminders but with lists of telephone numbers and names of animals that needed re-homing. In one notebook she wrote: 'Please make 1986 a happy year for all our animals at present in care. Dogs, cats, puppies all in urgent need of a home.' Mum wasn't interested in personal accolade, even though in 1993, and deservedly so, she was nominated for Cumbria Woman of the Year.

But this tough work was taking its toll. I remember that during the last year or two, during the hot summer months, Mum occasionally suffered blackouts. Whether she was simply too hot and dehydrated (the house still lacked insulation so heat easily penetrated the roof and walls), or this was a result of the migraines she'd always suffered from, or low blood pressure, I'm not sure. I would get telephone calls from Tom telling me he'd found her on the sitting room floor and I'd have to wait for Steve to return home from work before I could get to her. We worried about this, and about her increasing forgetfulness. Despite these problems, and although she rarely left her animals for more than an afternoon, in 1985 Mum decided to take herself off on a package holiday to La Spezia, Italy.

A package holiday seemed a wonderful idea as she didn't have to worry about transport or hotel bookings etc., everything was taken care of. So off she went and was having a marvellous time visiting beautiful ancient sites when one day she collapsed.

'It was as if I was being pulled to the ground,' she recalled. 'I felt terribly dizzy and sick. No one helped me, I think they thought I was drunk.' It must have been awful being on her own so far away from home. When she returned she went for tests to discover that she had Ménière's Disease – a rare disorder that affects the inner ear and can cause hearing loss. Having to take pills was bad enough for Mum but not being allowed to drive was a disaster –it meant that she was unable to collect animals, go shopping, do anything except stay at home. Seriously annoyed, she fought hard against this imprisonment. Losing her freedom was not on the agenda! It was around this time that she told me running the cafe was too draining. There was also more trouble with

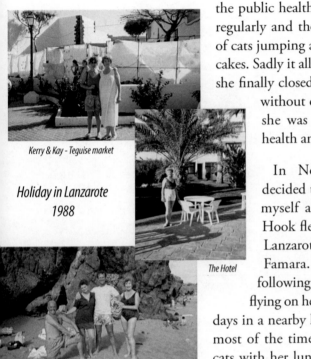

Kerry & Kay - Teguise market

Holiday in Lanzarote
1988

The Hotel

Derek Hook, Naomi, Steve & Kay on Playa Blanca

the public health inspector who called regularly and thoroughly disapproved of cats jumping around the scones and cakes. Sadly it all proved too much and she finally closed the café. After a year without dizziness or blackouts, she was given a clean bill of health and able to drive again.

In November 1988, we decided to cheer her up. Steve, myself and our friend Derek Hook flew off for a holiday in Lanzarote. We hired a villa in Famara. Mum joined us the following week. She coped well flying on her own and enjoyed ten days in a nearby hotel, where she spent most of the time feeding all the stray cats with her lunches and dinners – as always, putting the animals first. The holiday was just the tonic Mum needed.

Once home, we helped where we could. She seemed to lose her confidence in driving, and we tried to persuade her to use taxis. I took her shopping, for coffee and lunches which she enjoyed. More hospital visits in Kendal followed. On one of these occasions I remember the consultant asking her these questions: 'Who is the Prime Minister? When did World War Two break out? What year were you born?' She would look to me for the answers and I felt terrible not being allowed to help. Shortly afterwards she was taken to Preston Hospital for a brain scan and was diagnosed with Alzheimer's. It was a shock. She thought she would no longer be able to fulfil her role in Animal Concern.

But she soldiered on. Sometimes she would talk to me about how she couldn't remember things or hold decent conversations anymore; or whether she'd taken her medication that day. I would assure her that she'd had a lot to remember over the years and not to worry too much as that might make things worse. The local nurse gave her a 'dossette box' – a pill organiser, so she could take them correctly.

Over the next few years Mum became unsteady on her feet, more confused, and found it increasingly difficult to handle all the demands of Animal Concern – requests, letters, call-outs, meetings etc. In August 1997, reluctantly and with great sorrow, she handed over her position as Vice President.' The management committee at the time were: Brigadier C.E. Tryon-Wilson, C.B.E., D.S.O., D.L., President; Mr G. Harrison, F.R.I.C.S., Chairman; Miss L. Lockney, Vice Chairman; Mr. J. Hewitson, Hon. Treasurer; Mrs. M.P. Kenyon, Hon. Secretary. They too were very sad to see her go after all the incredibly hard work and all she'd accomplished throughout the years. Mum had succeeded in saving thousands of animals and even though she no longer attended meetings, her love and devotion to Animal Concern never ended.

The following years weren't easy for Mum. She was not one to give up, but the frustration of physically being unable to tackle most everyday things without help gradually got her down.

* * *

Amongst some of Mum's photos I'm looking through today, I find some of Steve and me and our two daughters when we lived at Crook near Kendal. They bring back a certain memory. I remember that time in 1972, when out of the blue, Mum handed me a letter. I was thrilled to see it was from Dad. After years of official separation, Mum had obviously decided I could, if I wished, contact him again and could make up my own mind about him. She certainly had no intention of picking up the old thread, but I did.

I hadn't seen Dad since I stayed with him in Blackheath in 1964. I was so excited to receive his letter. He told me he'd been living in Lytham St. Annes with a lady and that he wasn't a well man and I would find a great change in him. I replied with all our news about our children and where we lived. It was the best day ever when he drove up to see us. And yes, he was slower, looked a little flushed and had put on weight, but all I thought about at that moment was us being together again. We hugged and I smelled the warmth I remembered. We were thrilled to see each other again and my children adored him.

Steve and I kept up contact and returned visits to his little flat in Lytham to spend time with him and his lovely partner, who I could see made him very happy. But he obviously had regrets. He told Steve how sorry he was for his bad behaviour towards his family, how the war had traumatised him to the point of drinking heavily, beyond his control. For me, this was the moment I understood the terrible truth, when I realised why Mum and he were at loggerheads most of the time, and how helpless he felt.

In the winter of 1976, we were too busy moving house and saw very little of him. I really wanted Dad to see our old farmhouse tucked under Whinfell but it was too late. In early February, we received a phone call from his lady to say Dad had died.

I was nervous about telling Mum this awful news as I didn't know how she'd react. I invited her to our house for lunch and waited until we'd finished eating, then I told her. She said nothing, just promptly got up and walked out into the garden.

CHAPTER TWENTY-NINE

HAPPY 80th BIRTHDAY

Mum's birthday celebrations began when Steve and I drove her up to Edinburgh for a surprise concert. She had no idea where we were going. On May 1st 1997 at 7.30 p.m., we arrived at the Queens Hall where Nicholas Ashton, now Senior Lecturer at Edinburgh Napier University, was giving a piano recital. He played Beethoven, Schubert, Schumann and Brahms – all Mum's favourites. It was a beautiful and memorable evening. I was moved to see her almost speechless with joy and so proud of how brilliantly Nicholas's career had developed. They were both thrilled to see each other again after so many years. We said our goodbyes and after spending the night in a B & B, we drove her home. We then held a lunch party for her at the Rothay Hotel, Ambleside with all her family and friends. It went very well and Mum enjoyed every moment. She loved celebrations and they didn't end there. On 17th May, Judith and I took her to the Royal Festival Hall, London to hear Delius's *A Mass of Life*. The concert was held in memory of Eric Fenby, Delius's amanuensis in his latter years at Grez-sur-Loing – 'offering his services to his fellow-Yorkshireman.'

The next event we planned for her was a balloon ride, which the family had clubbed together to buy. As soon as weather conditions were suitable later that summer, up, up and away she slowly rose with her grandson Sean Tomlinson.

Kay's birthday balloon ride above Windermere

They set off from Lakeside and slowly glided over the treetops above Lake Windermere. She was overjoyed and thought it marvellous to see the bird's eye view of the fells she'd known and walked.

Kay's 80th birthday cake

Finally, I took Mum by train north to St Andrews, Scotland, for a re-union dinner at her old boarding school, St Leonards. She had a lovely time showing me around the rooms. We stayed in a little B & B near the shore and after breakfast we walked to the golf links where she remembered her father had played many times.

I was becoming acutely aware that these occasions were to be savoured: Mum was tiring and soon wouldn't be up to travelling. Fewer friends were calling to see her because they'd either died or were living too far away. Roy, who by then was married to Steve's sister Elizabeth, often called in at Rosewood on his way to Ambleside. Kathleen Phelan wrote long wonderful letters and sometimes dropped in on her way to or from Bolivia, Argentina, New York, The World. Mum was always pleased to see and hear about her escapades on the road. But when I asked who'd been to see her, sadly she often couldn't remember, though I saw from the number of used cups that tea had been brewed for someone.

CHAPTER THIRTY

FALLING

Tom, Judith's husband, still managed Mum's garden at Rosewood and kept an eye on everything. He often telephoned us if he was worried or something had happened to her. Mum would spend most sunny afternoons on her swing seat by the river snoozing and watching the sun setting behind the pines. I called to see her twice a week to

Listening to the sound of the river, 2005

take her shopping, for lunch, tea or for drives over Kirkstone or Little Langdale via Blea Tarn to Great Langdale. She loved being amongst the mountains again. If the weather was good, we would stop for her to sit on a boulder and gaze over at the Pikes. 'I can imagine walking up there, Kim running ahead,' she once said. I wanted more than anything else for her to be able to do that. Some days she didn't feel like going out and we'd sit together in front of a roaring fire drinking endless cups of coffee and watching television. I was taken aback when one wet afternoon whilst watching *To the Manor Born* on television when she suddenly announced, 'Oh, that's your Dad's first wife.' She was referring to Daphne Heard, who played the part of Maria Polouvicka, alias Mrs Poo, Peter Bowles' mother in the series. That was the first I knew of Dad's previous marriage. I have since tried to trace this fact with no result, but my South African cousins assure me that it is true.

Mum enjoyed short walks through the woods with her dogs, Bob, Beauty and Chippy who was blind, until one day someone on the opposite bank spotted her on the ground unable to get up. He rushed over the bridge to her rescue and helped her back home. Much to her annoyance she wasn't able to walk along that path again as the ground had eroded and become too rough. Whenever I visited, I took the dogs out, until finally they refused to go anywhere without Mum.

Rosewood in sunshine 2004

Rosewood in the snow 2004

Carers from Coniston called in twice a day to see that she was managing. One morning they couldn't get into the house and telephoned me. When I arrived, I climbed through a window and found Mum on her bedroom floor very cold and confused. We called an ambulance and she was taken into Kendal hospital. Mum was a fighter, but as I walked her slowly around the hospital ward, she found it hard to breathe and had pain in her shoulders and back. We visited her once or twice each day and even took her old Bob to see her in the hospital lobby. While we were there, she turned to Naomi and said; 'Why does everyone in here know I've got Alzheimer's except me?'

Social Services made an appointment to visit Rosewood to assess whether she could return home or would need proper nursing care. Even after taping down lino and removing obstacles, sadly, it was the latter. I looked into employing a private nurse but no one was prepared to live in the house with the animals. We had to think quickly what to do next. We made an appointment to view Hollow Oak Nursing Home at Haverthwaite.

My first question to them was 'Do you have any animals here?' When the reply was yes, remembering that Steve's mother had spent a happy two years there, we took the room. I drove Mum directly from hospital to Hollow Oak. The nurses were wonderful. She began eating and sleeping properly and appeared to take to her new surroundings very well, but she kept asking, 'When am I going home? Please can I go to my little shack by the river?'

I didn't think Mum would notice the changes we'd made to the house and yet the minute she went through the front door for the first time since she left, she looked down and said, 'New lino?' She was having a good day and noticed. She walked through the rooms inspecting everything. I wondered what she was thinking. I made some strong coffee, just how she liked it, and we sat by the river. I watched her eyes close listening to the sounds and memories running through.

I got used to my new role of decision-making but sometimes Mum appeared to be suspicious of what might be going on behind her back. I learned gradually how to handle her Alzheimer's and knew if I diverted her thoughts and made her laugh she would be calmed and fine.

During the following months Patrick, Judith and their children came regularly to Rosewood for holidays. I would report to Mum who'd stayed in the house, which pleased her. She knew the house was still alive.

Judith, Patrick, Kay & Kerry in the back garden at Rosewood, 2005

I've lost track of time until I hear rain pelting the roof and notice how dark it's become. Hours engulfed by fragments of Mum's life. I've sorted almost everything except for this last damp box. I heave it out from the back of the wardrobe. There are diaries on the top and tucked near the bottom underneath I find a few writings. They look like very old poems, typed on soft thin paper. I read the first one, signed 'Barry Callaghan':

" A Song of Love."

Then come my dear, let's leave this world of cares
And shady Sorrows,
Forget all thoughts and stupid fears
For dull To-Morrows;
And ride in a shining fairy boat, whose full sail gleams
Vividly white,
Away to the Island of Love's tender Dreams
Thro' the pale moonlight.
Breast to breast, body to body we'll lie
With sweet emotion,
While a soft refreshing breeze whispers by
From the murmuring Ocean.
There let us stay till the latest breath
Leaves us and we die; -
Yet still united, in the Arms of Death
We'll lie.

----------oOo----------

Barry Callaghan,

I read the second which is in Mum's handwriting:

Curious, I roll and tie the poems with red ribbon and tuck them in a drawer. I will have to choose the right moment to ask Mum about these.

A little circle of lamp & firelight,
A perfect blending of words & thoughts,
A fusion of mind & body,
A feeling so deep, a music so rare,
As the amber flow of a river.
The warm glow of fire on skin, hair,
& eyes,
So many unspoken words, so well
understood;
This moment in time, I will remember

Chapter Thirty-One

IN DREAMS

It was Christmas 2004 when all the family returned to stay at Rosewood. We collected Mum in the morning from Hollow Oak. Judith cooked a wonderful turkey lunch which Mum ate heartily. After a small glass of her latest favourite tipple, Dubonnet, she snoozed peacefully in her chair by the fire. It was like old times, our family together, but I worried about how we would broach the subject of driving her back to Hollow Oak. At around 5 o'clock she turned to me and said, 'I think it's time I was going back now.' I was relieved; she had accepted.

We spent the next months visiting her as often as we could, taking her out for lunches or afternoon tea. I made a point of driving Mum out to different places so she could look at the hills. She slept most of the time but would wake and remark on the lake or beautiful trees. I know she loved trees but also knew she was still being considerate, showing her appreciation, always thinking of other people.

One sunny August day we arranged for her brother Berwick and wife Joanna, her sister Joan and son David to have lunch together at the Lakeside Hotel, Newby Bridge. All three siblings suffering from Alzheimer's, their conversation went

Kay, Berwick & Joan outside Hollow Oak Nursing Home 2004

round and round, none of them remembering what each had just said. It mattered little as everything was about enjoying 'the moment.' Auntie Joan asked if the music could be turned down. A difficult request for a live pianist! The hotel staff were very understanding and fortunately found this amusing, in fact they were in fits of laughter. Days like that seemed to be a tonic for Mum.

Judith, Kay & Kerry raising a birthday glass of Pimms at The Lakeside Hotel, 2005

Some weeks later, when I arrived at Hollow Oak to see Mum, she couldn't wait to tell me a dream she'd had. This was very unusual, she never talked about the dreams she'd had. It sounded typically jumbled – in the way some dreams are:

'I was at home, in bed. I could hear a party going on in the sitting room next door. A lot of voices I knew, all my friends, but I was unable to get through to them. And then, there was this book in the road.'

'What book, Mum? What was in the book?'

'No, nothing, I turned the pages but it was empty.'

'Was there anything else you remember?'

'No, just the book in the road.' Mum spoke no more about it but I was intrigued. When I mentioned this months later to my friend Anne, she suggested I might think about filling the empty pages.

Bonfire night was clear and crisp. I got the urge to go and see Mum. Hollow Oak always celebrated occasions, and when Steve and I arrived the residents were gathered in the sitting room watching fireworks through the window. Mum sat close holding my hand. She nodded as if approving each fantastic display. When the last sparkle had died down Tony started talking about Christmas, all the parties and entertainment they were going to enjoy. Mum said nothing. She looked very tired so I wheeled her back to her room. We chatted for a few minutes then I took a deep breath and pulled out the rolled-up papers from my bag.

Kay in her room at Hollow Oak

'Mum, do you remember these?' I handed her the poems. She didn't untie the ribbon, just held them and looking out of the window into the night, whispered, 'Yes, it was a very long time ago.'

* * *

52 years later!
Judith, Kerry, Sheila & Patrick back on the steps at Rosewood - 2004

We're planning to go over to Rosewood this morning to check there are no burst pipes, but just as we're leaving, a nurse from Hollow Oak telephones to tell me that Mum is very poorly. I quickly pack some overnight things and Steve and I rush over to Hollow Oak. She's lying in bed, in and out of sleep, pale and elegant as a swan. She recognises us and is pleased we're there. I ask the nurse if there's anything we can do for her. She tells me that the doctor has been to check her and placed a morphine patch on her arm, she's not been eating and is very tired. Throughout the day we read magazines and passages from one of her favourite stories by Gerald Durrell, My Family and Other Animals. We play her favourite music – Frank Sinatra, Chopin, Debussy and, of course, Delius. Occasionally she opens her eyes and smiles. She's comfortable. I telephone the family and within a few hours Patrick and Judith are by her bedside. They talk to her and stroke her forehead. She's weak but occasionally smiles and nods in acknowledgement. It's late – nearly eleven o'clock – so they say their goodbyes and return to Rosewood for the night.

I sit in the gentle light close to her bed watching her. She breathes slowly and deeply. I try to warm her cold slender hands in mine and whisper all the things I hope will comfort her; stories of her animals, old friends, Rosewood and the river. Outside the sky is bright with stars and frost settling on the fields.

Acknowledgements

Thank you Mum for your courage, our happy 'interview' days and for leaving stacks of old papers, theatre reviews, letters, diaries and photos.

Thanks to Hunter Davies and The Cumbria Community Foundation for awarding me the Bursary in 2013, which helped enormously towards funding research, editing and formatting this biography.

Thanks to Liz Nuttall at Handstand Press for believing in and publishing my story.

Thanks to all those who researched and helped me with their recollections of Mum:

My sister, Judith Tomlinson and my brother, Patrick Callaghan for their childhood experiences and encouraging me to write this book.

Phyllis Ashton, Mum's life-long friend who remembered in great detail their early days together.

Nicholas Ashton for the lovely letter to me remembering his first meeting with Mum and Rosewood in 1972.

Roy Brown, my brother in law, for his friendship and amusing anecdotes.

Gordon and Barbara Fox for their friendship and musical years at Rosewood.

Auntie Joan Smith for her brilliant recollections of their early life.

My daughters Rebecca and Naomi for their childhood memories of Granny.

Andrew Smith for memories of our golfing Grandfather, Alfred, 'Smiter'.

Berwick Smith for his early family photographs

Sheila Ogden for giving me her side of the story from across the road at Greenbank and divulging the villagers' first impressions of their new neighbour.

Chris Callaghan for details about his father Barry Callaghan in his book *They Came from Afar.*

Jane Renouf for her Gazette reviews and memories of Mum in the Ambleside Players.

Madge Wadecar who kindly provided all the Ambleside Players information.

Dr. Anne Mathieson for indicating that the empty *'book in the road'* needed filling, and for reading through.

Kay Phelan for writing her pamphlets and who, regardless of a life on the road, lived to the grand age of 97.

Clare Delius for her book *Frederick Delius: Memories of my brother.*

Joanna Blatchley for the theatre research.

Joan Whitworth for school days memories.

Jo Moon for the Animal Rescue years.

James Thornton, Library Manager at RADA, 8 Chenies St., London. WC1E 7PA.

The Westmorland Gazette Archives.

Professor Grevel Lindop for editing.

And finally Steve, who read draft after draft with such enthusiasm